MW01089470

UCLA
Los Angeles, California

Written by Erik Robert Flegal

Edited by Adam Burns, Kimberly Moore, and Jon Skindzier

Layout by Matt Hamman

*Additional contributions by Omid Gohari,
Christina Koshzow, Chris Mason, Joey Rahimi,
and Luke Skurman*

ISBN # 1-4274-0158-6
ISSN # 1552-0927
© Copyright 2006 College Prowler
All Rights Reserved
Printed in the U.S.A.
www.collegeprowler.com

Last updated: 7/07/08

Special Thanks To: Babs Carryer, Andy Hannah, LaunchCyte, Tim O'Brien, Bob Sehlinger, Thomas Emerson, Andrew Skurman, Barbara Skurman, Bert Mann, Dave Lehman, Daniel Fayock, Chris Babyak, The Donald H. Jones Center for Entrepreneurship, Terry Slease, Jerry McGinnis, Bill Ecenberger, Idie McGinty, Kyle Russell, Jacque Zaremba, Larry Winderbaum, Roland Allen, Jon Reider, Team Evankovich, Lauren Varacalli, Abu Noaman, Mark Exler, Daniel Steinmeyer, Jared Cohon, Gabriela Oates, David Koegler, and Glen Meakem.

Bounce-Back Team: John Liu, Mikel Freemon, Shannon Mo, Robert Jue, Jenny Kim, and David Chen.

College Prowler®
5001 Baum Blvd.
Suite 750
Pittsburgh, PA 15213

Phone: 1-800-290-2682
Fax: 1-800-772-4972
E-Mail: info@collegeprowler.com
Web Site: www.collegeprowler.com

College Prowler® is not sponsored by, affiliated with, or approved by UCLA in any way.

College Prowler® strives faithfully to record its sources. As the reader understands, opinions, impressions, and experiences are necessarily personal and unique. Accordingly, there are, and can be, no guarantees of future satisfaction extended to the reader.

© Copyright 2006 College Prowler. All rights reserved. No part of this work may be reproduced or transmitted in any form or by any means, including but not limited to, photocopy, recording, or any information storage and retrieval systems, without the express written permission of College Prowler®.

How this all started...

When I was trying to find the perfect college, I used every resource that was available to me. I went online to visit school websites; I talked with my high school guidance counselor; I read book after book; I hired a private counselor. Sure, this was all very helpful, but nothing really told me what life was like at the schools I cared about. These sources weren't giving me enough information to be totally confident in my decision.

In all my research, there were only two ways to get the information I wanted.

The first was to physically visit the campuses and see if things were really how the brochures described them, but this was quite expensive and not always feasible. The second involved a missing ingredient: the students. Actually talking to a few students at those schools gave me a taste of the information that I needed so badly. The problem was that I wanted more but didn't have access to enough people.

In the end, I weighed my options and decided on a school that felt right and had a great academic reputation, but truth be told, the choice was still very much a crapshoot. I had done as much research as any other student, but was I 100 percent positive that I had picked the school of my dreams?

Absolutely not.

My dream in creating *College Prowler* was to build a resource that people can use with confidence. My own college search experience taught me the importance of gaining true insider insight; that's why the majority of this guide is composed of quotes from actual students. After all, shouldn't you hear about a school from the people who know it best?

I hope you enjoy reading this book as much as I've enjoyed putting it together. Tell me what you think when you get a chance. I'd love to hear your college selection stories.

Luke Skurman
CEO and Co-Founder
lukeskurman@collegeprowler.com

Welcome to College Prowler®

During the writing of College Prowler's guidebooks, we felt it was critical that our content was unbiased and unaffiliated with any college or university. We think it's important that our readers get honest information and a realistic impression of the student opinions on any campus—that's why if any aspect of a particular school is terrible, we (unlike a campus brochure) intend to publish it. While we do keep an eye out for the occasional extremist—the cheerleader or the cynic—we take pride in letting the students tell it like it is. We strive to create a book that's as representative as possible of each particular campus. Our books cover both the good and the bad, and whether the survey responses point to recurring trends or a variation in opinion, these sentiments are directly and proportionally expressed through our guides.

College Prowler guidebooks are in the hands of students throughout the entire process of their creation. Because you can't make student-written guides without the students, we have students at each campus who help write, randomly survey their peers, edit, layout, and perform accuracy checks on every book that we publish. From the very beginning, student writers gather the most up-to-date stats, facts, and inside information on their colleges. They fill each section with student quotes and summarize the findings in editorial reviews. In addition, each school receives a collection of letter grades (A through F) that reflect student opinion and help to represent contentment, prominence, or satisfaction for each of our 20 specific categories. Just as in grade school, the higher the mark the more content, more prominent, or more satisfied the students are with the particular category.

Once a book is written, additional students serve as editors and check for accuracy even more extensively. Our bounce-back team—a group of randomly selected students who have no involvement with the project—are asked to read over the material in order to help ensure that the book accurately expresses every aspect of the university and its students. This same process is applied to the 200-plus schools College Prowler currently covers. Each book is the result of endless student contributions, hundreds of pages of research and writing, and countless hours of hard work. All of this has led to the creation of a student information network that stretches across the nation to every school that we cover. It's no easy accomplishment, but it's the reason that our guides are such a great resource.

When reading our books and looking at our grades, keep in mind that every college is different and that the students who make up each school are not uniform—as a result, it is important to assess schools on a case-by-case basis. Because it's impossible to summarize an entire school with a single number or description, each book provides a dialogue, not a decision, that's made up of 20 different topics and hundreds of student quotes. In the end, we hope that this guide will serve as a valuable tool in your college selection process. Enjoy!

OMID GOHARI ◯ CHRISTINA KOSHZOW ◯ CHRIS MASON ◯ JOEY RAHIMI ◯ LUKE SKURMAN ◯
The College Prowler Team

Table of Contents

Introduction from the Author

Amid the sprawling suburbs of Los Angeles, and tucked away in one of the most glamorous neighborhoods, lies a university that adds even more allure to the already rich traditions of the city. The University of California-Los Angeles (UCLA) is a world-renowned institution with joint campuses planted in over 35 different countries around the globe, and professors that are so knowledgeable in their fields that some have even received the Nobel Prize.

Located in the filmmaking capital of the world, there are movie premieres weekly in the adjacent town of Westwood. The warm weather beckons students to venture outside to study year round, and the prime location offers students a quick escape from their studies to one of the local beaches for a quick dip in the Pacific Ocean. UCLA's strong athletic program, with some of the most notable national-championship teams in recent history, also helped to make the school such an internationally-respected institution.

The University is growing, and the diverse student body only helps the campus flourish. The diverse mix of students fits well into a University that houses five different schools of study, from Letters and Science to Arts and Architecture. Here in the melting pot of Los Angeles, under the guidance of intense professors, and surrounded by many other brilliant, young minds, creativity blossoms and students grow intellectually both inside and outside of the classroom.

There is a longstanding tradition of hard work and dedication at UCLA. Much of the student body requires financial aid and hold jobs simultaneously while taking classes. The resourcefulness of students at UCLA has grown throughout the years as college costs have increased and academic standards at the school have skyrocketed. Many professors note that there is a difference between the public-school student who has to make him or herself heard in the crowded lecture hall versus the private-school student who has smaller classes and does not have to grapple for that same attention. The difference is that at a public school like UCLA, students have to take the initiative in their classes much like people need to take initiative in real life to achieve certain goals. Students need to be resourceful and work harder to gain their professors attention, and there is definitely something to be said of the person that can meet that challenge at an institution as rigorous as UCLA.

Erik Robert Flegal, Author
UCLA

By the Numbers

General Information

UCLA
405 Hilgard Ave.
Los Angeles, CA 90095

Control:
Public

Academic Calendar:
Quarter

Religious Affiliation:
None

Founded:
1919

Web Site:
www.ucla.edu

Main Phone:
(310) 825-4321

Student Body

Full-Time Undergraduates:
24,931

Part-Time Undergraduates:
997

**Total Male
Undergraduates:**
11,579

**Total Female
Undergraduates:**
14,349

Admissions

Overall Acceptance Rate:
24%

**Early Decision
Acceptance Rate:**
Not offered

**Early Action
Acceptance Rate:**
Not offered

Regular Acceptance Rate:
24%

Total Applicants:
50,755

Total Acceptances:
11,963

Freshman Enrollment:
4,564

Yield (admitted students who actually enroll):
38%

Regular Decision Deadline:
November 30

**Regular Decision
Notification:**
March 31

Must Reply-By Date:
May 1

**Applicants Placed on
Waiting List:**
Not offered

**Transfer Applications
Received:**
13,451

**Transfer Applications
Accepted:**
5,330

Transfer Students Enrolled:
3,321

**Transfer Application
Acceptance Rate:**
40%

SAT I or ACT Required?
Yes, either

**SAT I Range
(25th–75th Percentile):**
1360–1480

**SAT I Verbal Range
(25th–75th Percentile):**
660–720

**SAT I Math Range
(25th–75th Percentile):**
700–760

SAT II Requirements:
Writing, Math, and any other
SAT II of your choice

Retention Rate:
97%

**Top 10% of
High School Class:**
97%

**Common Application
Accepted?**
No

Supplemental Forms?
No

Application Fee:
$60

Admissions Phone:
(310) 825-3101

Admissions E-Mail:
ugadm@saonet.ucla.edu

Admissions Web Site:
www.admissions.ucla.edu

Financial Information

In-State Tuition:
$7,038

Out-of-State Tuition:
$27,027

Registration Fee:
$40 per semester

Room and Board:
$12,420

Books and Supplies:
$1,515 per year

Average Need-Based Financial Aid Package (including loans, work-study, and other sources):
$14,329

Students Who Applied For Financial Aid:
55%

Applicants Who Received Aid:
90%

Financial Aid Forms Deadline:
March 2

Financial Aid Phone:
(310) 206-0400

Financial Aid E-Mail:
finaid@saonet.ucla.edu

Financial Aid Web Site:
www.fao.ucla.edu

Academics

The Lowdown On...
Academics

Degrees Awarded:
Bachelor's
Master's
Doctorate
First Professional

Most Popular Majors:
27% Social sciences
13% Psychology
12% Biological/life sciences
8% History
6% English

Undergraduate Schools:
College of Letters and Sciences
Samueli School of Engineering and Applied Science
School of the Arts and Architecture
School of Nursing
School of Theater, Film, and Television

Full-Time Faculty:
1,948

Faculty with Terminal Degree:
98%

Student-to-Faculty Ratio:
16:1

Average Course Load:
16 credits (4 courses)

Class Sizes:
Fewer than 20 Students: 54%
20 to 49 Students: 26%
50 or More Students: 20%

Graduation Rates:
Four-Year: 66%
Five-Year: 88%
Six-Year: 90%

Special Degree Options

Accelerated program, distance learning, double major, English as a Second Language (ESL), honors program, independent study, internships, liberal arts/career combination, student-designed major, study abroad

AP Test Score Requirements

Possible credit for scores of 3 to 5
Class credit for scores of 4 or 5

IB Test Score Requirements

Possible credit for scores of 6 or 7

Sample Academic Clubs

An association for each undergraduate major, Golden Key, Mortar Board, Student Alumni Association

Best Places to Study:

The Powell Library Dungeon, fourth and fifth floors of the Young Research Library, on the hill next to the Jan's Steps

Did You Know?

You can **create your own major** by running it over with your counselor and pushing through a lot of red tape. Some of these majors catch on and become entrenched in the curriculum like the new international development major.

Students Speak Out On...
Academics

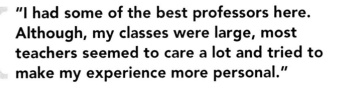

"I had some of the best professors here. Although, my classes were large, most teachers seemed to care a lot and tried to make my experience more personal."

Q "Language classes are particularly good. Admittedly, **some professors are more concerned with their research than with teaching an undergrad class**. But for big lectures, the University tends to hire excellent lecturers."

Q "The professors really vary. I've had some horrendous ones that don't care about undergrads and are only interested in their research, and I have had some brilliant and encouraging professors, as well. As you get to upper-division courses, the professors get better, and the classes are more personal. Due to the nature of the school, though, it's hard to get to know teachers on a one-on-one basis. **They just go through too many of us too quickly** with the quarters being only 10 weeks long."

Q "I had mostly science teachers. I had several teachers that were enthusiastic about their subject of expertise making the class both interesting and informative. Of course, **some were boring and others incoherent**; I swear one was 127 years old."

Q "The professors aren't so bad; it all depends on your major. Sometimes, you'll get a really cool professor, and once in a while, you'll get stuck with a totally crappy one. All I have to say is that **the professor you get for a class makes a huge difference** on whether or not you'll do well in the class or whether the class is actually worthwhile."

Q "They cover the whole range from very good to very bad. I've probably had more mediocre/poor professors than good professors. Many are preoccupied with their own research and put minimal effort into teaching, and some are simply old and disorganized and unable to convey the material. On the other hand, I have also had several excellent teachers who go above and beyond the course requirements, put in a lot of extra time and effort into the class, and give very good lecturers. One more thing, **a good TA is exceedingly rare in the sciences**; most are hard to understand and not very helpful."

Q "**The teachers here come in a wide variety**. Some are boring; some are fun. Some are easy; some are hard. I haven't had many problems with my professors, but that's just me. We have a Web site where you can look up other students' comments about a particular professor and rate his or her performance, *www.uclaprofessors.com*."

Q "I've fortunately had great experiences with most of my professors. One, however, was terrible. He was out for half the quarter, and **we hardly learned anything**, yet we were tested on all of the materials that we had to 'study.'"

The College Prowler Take On...
Academics

The teachers at UCLA are qualified, as many of them earned their graduate degrees at some of the most prestigious American colleges, including the Ivy Leagues. Many of the professors are so involved that they've devoted their lives to their subjects, and not to teaching. However, many professors cannot communicate their innovative ideas clearly enough in one quarter of a class. Luckily, most of them are available for office hours at least two or three times a week. Contrary to popular belief, most of the professors at UCLA want to help the students in their classes, but for the most part, the student will have to make the first step.

The quality of professors at UCLA is so sporadic that students cannot help but be a bit skeptic upon selecting courses. Yes, the professors are knowledgeable, but there is no set way to know a professor's style of teaching, or how much the professor cares about student learning. The only thing concrete regarding academics at UCLA is that the deeper a student descends into a major, the more attentive and enriching the professors become. There are fewer teaching assistants (TAs) in the upper-division classes, especially on North Campus. Information on professors is pretty easy to find, and it helps to tap multiple sources to create a fuller image of a professor. You can always check out *www.uclaprofessors.com*, a Web site that lets the students grade the professors. For the most part, the reviews you'll find here are accurate, even though the teachers and advisors may tell you otherwise.

The College Prowler® Grade on
Academics: A-

A high Academics grade generally indicates that professors are knowledgeable, accessible, and genuinely interested in their students' welfare. Other determining factors include class size, how well professors communicate, and whether or not classes are engaging.

Local Atmosphere

The Lowdown On...
Local Atmosphere

Region:
West Coast

City, State:
Los Angeles, CA

Setting:
Large metropolitan city

Distance from San Diego:
2 hours

Distance to San Francisco:
6 hours, 30 minutes

Points of Interest:
Bel Air (Star Homes)
Beverly Hills (Rodeo Drive)
Disneyland
Hollywood
Malibu and surrounding beaches
Sunset Strip
Venice Beach

Movie Theaters:

AMC Avco Cinema
10840 Wilshire Blvd.
Los Angeles
(310) 475-0711

Mann Festival Theater
10887 Lindbrook Dr.
Westwood
(310) 208-4575

Mann Village and Mann Bruin
961 Broxton Ave.
Los Angeles
(310) 208-0018

Major Sports Teams:

Dodgers (baseball)
Lakers (basketball)
Clippers (basketball)
Kings (hockey)

Theme Parks:

Disneyland/California Adventure
1313 S. Harbor Blvd.
Anaheim
(714) 781-4000

Knotts Berry Farm
8039 Beach Blvd.
Buena Park
(714) 220-5200

Magic Mountain
26101 Magic Mountain Pkwy.
Valencia
(818) 367-5965

Universal Studios
100 Universal City Plaza
Universal City
(800) UNIVERSAL

City Web Sites

www.ci.la.ca.us – Official city Web site

www.digitalcity.com/losangeles – Entertainment, food, and event picks for the city

www.losangeles.com – Entertainment and attractions guide

Did You Know?

5 Fun Facts about LA:

- Many famous actors and actresses live within a 15-minute drive of Hollywood Boulevard. **It's very likely you'll bump into a famous person** when touring the city and have a story to tell your friends back home.

- People trying to **hike to the Hollywood sign** can be arrested and serve jail time with a fine.

- **Almost every prominent actor has a star on the Hollywood Walk of Fame** on Hollywood Boulevard, and there are some extensions of this growing relic in Westwood.

- **Movie premiers erupt in Westwood biweekly**, so keep your ears open for a chance to catch the swanky red carpet strut of your favorite star!

- **The majority of the actors and actresses that you see are not originally from Los Angeles**. The majority are from other parts of America.

Famous Residents of LA:

Mark McGwire
Richard Nixon
George Patton
Robert Redford
Sally Ride
Adlai Stevenson
Venus and Serena Williams
Tiger Woods

Local Slang:

Coke – What a Los Angelino uses to refer to all carbonated beverages.

The Strip – The Sunset Strip.

Students Speak Out On...
Local Atmosphere

"LA's atmosphere is awesome. There are lots of other schools around the area, including USC. Boooooo!"

"**Los Angeles is a tourist's dream**; there are museums, amusement parks, water parks, movies, theater, musicals, beaches, and movie stars right outside your door."

"Westwood's atmosphere is a mixture of tourists and students who don't have cars. There are a couple of pretty nice theaters, where the premieres are actually held, and restaurants. I feel that **it isn't really college oriented because there aren't enough bars**, just expensive restaurants that students can't afford."

"**Westwood is a good college town**. There are lots of little shops, restaurants, coffee shops, and theaters. As for Los Angeles in general, there is everything from the beaches to Hollywood, all the clubs on Sunset, Disneyland, and Magic Mountain."

"UCLA is lucky to be right in the middle of it all. We are right next to Bel Air and Beverly Hills. Westwood is also the place for all the big Hollywood movie premieres. **There are good beaches, good shopping places, and not really any other universities close by**, although our rivals from USC like to come hang out."

Q "**The area directly adjacent to campus is for students**. There are many interesting things to do around the town including bars, clubs, museums, and the usual. Stay away from the Buck Fifty restaurant unless you like sitting on the toilet for hours at a time. The alley behind Maloney's is bad stuff, too."

Q "UCLA is right in Los Angeles. It's in a really nice area between Brentwood, Bel Air, and Beverly Hills. Santa Monica, Venice, West Hollywood, and the La Brea and Fairfax districts are all cool places to hang out. Hollywood, downtown, and South Central are worth skipping. There's **never a lack of things to do** in Los Angeles. That is, of course, if you have a car."

Q "Across town, you'll find our school rival: USC. Yep, those damn Trojans. Westwood's a pretty cool city for a while, but it gets boring after you've seen all the places. There are quite a few movie theaters in close vicinity, so that's always good. If you have people who drive, there are tons of places to go to in Los Angeles. **Activities in Southern California are endless, as long as you have transportation**."

Q "It's cheerful; everyone is nice and great. **There are five big universities by UCLA**. They are, by distance: Mt. St. Mary's in Brentwood, Loyola Marymount by LAX, CSUN in Northridge, USC near Downtown/South Central, and Pepperdine in Malibu. I'd stay away from South Central; it's a much better place than before the riots, but I wouldn't go there alone, especially at night. The same goes for Hollywood; if you go there during the day, that's fine; at night, go with friends. Other than that, the area is pretty cool."

The College Prowler Take On...
Local Atmosphere

Despite its reputation of being the capitol of face lifts and breast implants, Los Angeles actually has a casual style and many unique neighborhoods. Their are many patches of culture and fun scattered throughout the city. To get around Los Angeles and see everything that the city has to offer, a car is necessary. In the student-led life of Westwood, however, all you need is a pair of walking shoes and your student ID.

There are many other universities within a 20-minute drive: Loyola Marymount, Los Angeles State University, and of course our hated cross-town rival University of Southern California. Although these Universities are all close by, there is not much intermingling between the students because each neighborhood in LA, at times, feels like a separate universe. As for the UCLA galaxy, there are quite a few sights worth checking out that are only a short (free) bus ride away. With so many nightlife options at your fingertips, Los Angeles is one of the premiere spots in the entire country to party. You can hobnob with the stars, check out the assortment of bars and clubs, or take it easy and make it a Blockbuster night after watching a movie premiere. The fact that clubs close at 2 a.m. is a definite bummer. It is difficult to fully experience Los Angeles without owning a car. Yet, what truly leaves an impression about Los Angeles is the sheer endlessness of the city. One person can never "do it all."

The College Prowler® Grade on

Local Atmosphere: A+

A high Local Atmosphere grade indicates that the area surrounding campus is safe and scenic. Other factors include nearby attractions, proximity to other schools, and the town's attitude toward students.

Safety & Security

The Lowdown On...
Safety & Security

UCLA Police:
100 full-time police
120 student officers

UCLA Police Phone:
(310) 825-1491

Safety Services:
Blue-button emergency phones
Night campus vans
Night escort services

Health Center:
Arthur Ashe Student Health
and Wellness Center
Hours: Monday, Wednesday–
Friday 8 a.m.–6:30 p.m.,
Tuesday 9 a.m.–6:30 p.m.

Health Services:
Basic medical services
Counseling and psych services
On-site pharmaceuticals
Pregnancy and STD screening
X-rays

Did You Know?

In 1988, Access Control started because homeless people were living in the lounging areas between the north and south side of the dorms. **This service kept out the homeless and cut petty theft** in the dorms. Campus officials have worked hard to make students feel safe.

Students Speak Out On...
Safety & Security

"The security and safety on campus is pretty good. At night, there are community service officers biking around, and there is also an evening van service that takes you back to the dorms."

"I feel very safe on campus. I have lived in the dorms all four years and have never felt like my safety was in jeopardy. We have, however, had our share of security alerts. However, UCLA's police department, the UCPD, worked diligently to ensure campus safety. We have also had a prank caller in the dorms; however, the assailant was caught and punished appropriately. These were isolated incidents, though, and they never made me fear for my own safety. There are many security programs in place, like **evening vans that take you from campus to the dorms** at night and an escort service that will walk you home."

"Security is extremely safe. We have our own police department on campus and 'guards' patrol on foot and on bicycles. Vans come to designated spots regularly into the night. **One time, I even got handcuffed for talking to a guy**. Talk about safe!"

"The campus is pretty safe. **The UCPD does a good job of patrolling**, and we have a program of student cops on bikes for more presence and visibility. There's also an escort service available for those late study nights."

Q "I've never had any problems with safety at all. If at anytime you feel uncomfortable, you can call for someone to escort you back to the dorms. Like anywhere else, you must be cautious for your own safety. Make sure you know your surroundings, and if something funky is going on, you might want to call for help. As far as security for dorms goes, **after a certain time, there's limited access for people who don't live in that specific dorm**. Either way, to get into a dorm hall, you need your student ID."

Q "It's okay; there are campus security officers who think they're tough stuff. However, **there was a rapist a few years ago**, and people were afraid to leave their rooms for a few weeks."

Q "**I think that campus security does its job**. I've always felt safe and never really thought about security until right now. In all honesty, I hated the dorms because they were overly secure. Seriously, do you really need a monitor who's entering the building between 9 p.m. and 5 a.m.? One of the reasons that I left the dorms was because of the security. Nothing is going to happen at UCLA, nothing ever does."

Q "UCLA is located in Westwood, California, and is surrounded by million-dollar homes and offices. With all that money, the residents here can definitely afford the services of private security, so it's safe to assume that UCLA is really safe. There are campus officers patrolling all the time; you can't miss them. I personally think it's one of the safest places there is. Of course, **it's not wise to walk alone at night**; who knows what drunken, college guys will be willing to do."

Q "Here in LA, whenever you see mansions and huge houses, chances are **you are in a rich neighborhood and it's really safe**. We have the LAPD and the UCPD, too. If safety is one of your main concerns, you don't have to worry about it here. This is UCLA, not USC, you know?"

Q "There is a free campus escort service all night, every night, and they will walk you from wherever you are back to your residence. **There are security phones all over campus that connect you to the campus police**, too. I have never felt unsafe at UCLA. I have actually never felt the need to use any of these services, and I don't know anyone who did either. The campus and Westwood are pretty safe, but there are quite a few homeless people in Westwood who will ask you for money; that's about it."

The College Prowler Take On...
Safety & Security

The UCLA campus is one of the most secure in the UC system. UCLA employs its own police force, with officers that patrol the campus day and night. In the daytime, UCLA is extremely safe. Some people fall prey to petty theft, but for the most part, crime is not an issue. Although the campus does not have the same overall secure feel at night due to its size, there are several programs in place to keep students safe. Community Service Officers (CSO) are made up of a squad of students that form a police force that uses walkie-talkies in place of guns. They can walk you where you need to go after dark. Simply call 835-WALK, and a community service officer will swoop you up in 15 minutes or less for a walk home. Or if exercise is not on your agenda, you can always wait at any of the designated CSO van stops.

The dorms offer Access Control, a service made to deter non-residents from trying to enter the dorms from 9 p.m. to 5 a.m. Residents must swipe their ID card to enter a dorm during these hours and sign in non-resident guests to gain access. This is not the case in the suites, which are open to any visitor (or intruder, for that matter) who wishes to intrude. At least once a year, the suites are broken into, and two student-athletes were recently held at gunpoint for about $2,500 worth of merchandise. While acts of violence on campus are rare, they are definitely not out of the question on an urban campus such as UCLA's.

B+

The College Prowler® Grade on

Safety & Security: B+

A high grade in Safety & Security means that students generally feel safe, campus police are visible, blue-light phones and escort services are readily available, and safety precautions are not overly necessary.

Computers

The Lowdown On...
Computers

High-Speed Network?
Yes (Ethernet)

Wireless Network?
Yes, in designated areas throughout campus

Number of Labs:
16

Number of Computers:
939 PCs/139 Macs/180 Laptops

Operating Systems:
PC, Mac , and Linux

24-Hour Labs:
During the week before finals and finals week, Powell is open 24 hours.

Charge To Print:
Black and white: 3–25 cents
Color: 35–75 cents

Students Speak Out On...
Computers

"There are good, fast PCs and Macs in the dorms and on campus. The labs are always crowded, though, and you will definitely have to wait for a computer."

"As always, it's convenient to bring your own items with you, but you could live without your own computer if you had to. There are several computer labs on campus and in the dorms. You'll have to check out to see which times are not as busy. During lunch at Powell Library, it gets hectic in the CLICC lab, but you'll eventually be able to use it. As far as having a computer in the dorms goes, **there'll be so many people that live around you with computers that you seriously don't need your own**. Chances are your roommate will have one."

"**UCLA is very focused on technology**, and they spend a lot of money on it. There are many labs around campus, and the CLICC Lab in Powell Library is among the most crowded and popular. I recommend having a laptop. There are Ethernet ports in all the dorms and most everywhere on campus. A new wireless Ethernet program is still being tested."

"If you do not have a computer, there are at least 10 labs with accessible computers. **The school has its own servers so the connection is quite fast**. Bringing your own computer is even better because there are multiple ports in the dorm rooms and ports in the libraries."

Q "I would recommend bringing your own computer because in the dorms we have Ethernet. It's **really fast and convenient**. You need an Ethernet card and cable, but a lot of new computers these days have them installed already. The labs, as far as I know, aren't too crowded, as there are many available on campus and in the dorms, especially. However, some of these labs aren't open 24 hours; this impacts those last-minute all-nighters."

The College Prowler Take On...
Computers

At UCLA, computer labs are as plentiful as the California sunshine. Checking e-mail from any of the 17 labs usually requires no more than a five-minute wait. Now, finding a computer to use for more than five minutes is slightly more challenging. Students pack the CLICC Lab in the College Library where they can use both Macs and PCs to check e-mail in 10-minute increments, or use a computer for schoolwork up to two hours. However, the line is hefty between classes. Although there are many computers on campus to use, many are limited for use in a specific major. The wait for a computer in the main library can take an upwards of 20 minutes at lunchtime, and even then there is a two-hour usage limit. When there is not a class in session, the third floor of Powell is open for student use, and there is hardly ever a line. In order to find a complete listing of lab times, check out *www.computerlabs.ucla.edu*.

The libraries also have power plugs and Ethernet hookups accessible for students looking to study. The best bet for private usage of a computer is to pack it up with your sack lunch in the morning. Or better yet, check out a laptop from the CLICC Lab at Powell Library. That is a little known secret that will save money and time, all the while bringing peace of mind. Overall, computers are plentiful, but the labs still lack the freedom to snag the A grade. UCLA definitely deserves kudos for their computer network, but the grade below also reflects the fact that there just do not seem to be quite enough.

The College Prowler® Grade on

Computers: B+

A high grade in Computers designates that computer labs are available, the computer network is easily accessible, and the campus' computing technology is up-to-date.

Facilities

The Lowdown On...
Facilities

Student Center:
Ackerman Union

Athletic Center:
John Wooden Center

Libraries:
25

Campus Size:
419 acres

Popular Places to Chill:
Ackerman Union
The Bombshelter
The hill next to Jan's Steps
Northern Lights

What Is There to Do on Campus?

Between classes, you can soak up sun, grab some chow, sculpt a stellar body at the gym, or play a round of pool without walking more than one mile.

Movie Theater on Campus?

Melnitz Movies are screened at the James Bridges Theatre in Melnitz Hall and are free admission for UCLA students, faculty, and guests. Check the Web site for the complete list of Wednesday and Friday movie screenings. Pre-screenings of upcoming movies are available through Melnitz Movies, also. Call the Bridges Theater box office at (310) 206-8365 to reserve tickets. Also check out *gsa.asucla.ucla.edu/~melnitz*.

Bar on Campus?

No, but there are many right off campus in Westwood.

Coffeehouse on Campus?

Yes, there is the Northern Lights, Kerckhoff Coffee House, and LuValle Commons.

Favorite Things to Do

Free movie screenings are always full. The pre-screenings at UCLA are always packed regardless of how a movie is going to do at the box office. There are also events cooked up, from speakers to plays, at the North Campus Auditorium going on each week. Look for the cultural shows to really build momentum towards the end of the year when the squads get all their practice in. Also, everyday there is a show presented in Ackerman Square from 12 p.m. to 1 p.m.

Students Speak Out On...
Facilities

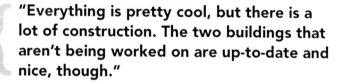

"Everything is pretty cool, but there is a lot of construction. The two buildings that aren't being worked on are up-to-date and nice, though."

Q "The administration makes a concerted effort to keep the facilities in good condition. The **campus is always amazingly clean**. Computer labs always have the latest software and hardware. The fitness center could use an expansion and an update in equipment, though. I couldn't stand going there, but I know others who did. The student center is new, but it's definitely not a center of student socialization."

Q "I like the gyms. I know that they tend to get crowded, but the best part about the free time between classes is hitting the gym. **The gym is so close and accessible that there is no way that people can't like it**. I go in to lift weights or check out a basketball and just shoot some hoops. It's a great way to meet people. I love it!"

Q "We have the Wooden Center, a state-of-the-art workout facility, complete with racquetball courts, a rock climbing wall, and basketball courts. UCLA has the privilege of being the only campus to offer the real **Tae-Bo taught by Billy Blanks' instructors**. It's seriously a good workout! The student center is called Ackerman Union and there's an arcade, a student store (complete with a Clinique counter!), many restaurants and lounges, and a whole bunch of meeting rooms."

Q "Computer labs are located in the many libraries on campus, but you'd probably want to go to Powell Library or Young Library to use a computer. A new feature that I like to use is **checking out laptops for two hours** and being able to take them out of the library. They are also testing out a new wireless Internet access, which seems pretty cool."

Q "The facilities are decent. **The gym is a little bit small for the size of the student body**, though. It expands in size and quality every year, though."

The College Prowler Take On...
Facilities

The facilities of UCLA follow the true UC spirit—Under Construction. The Wooden Center, the athletic gymnasium, is a true powerhouse with a weight room, three basketball courts, two volleyball courts, numerous racquetball courts, a rock climbing wall, a cardiovascular area, and private rooms that offer lessons in everything from martial arts to hip hop dance, and dance aerobics. Now that the renovation has subsided, the Wooden Center has even more aerobic rooms and a newly-installed locker room facility. The center is home to some physical, extreme pick-up basketball, especially in the summer when the professionals come to play. Some of the celebrities that enjoy UCLA's facilities enough to come back are Master P and Magic Johnson who both play pickup basketball from time to time in the summer.

The Wooden Center also offers an array of classes that span the interests of every undergraduate for a student price of around $30. The classes usually meet twice a week and last 10 weeks. Also worth looking into are the aquatic classes offered at the marina. The marina is about a 25-minute drive from the campus, but carpooling is available and the prices for these classes—rowing, scuba diving, and sailing—are competitive.

The College Prowler® Grade on
Facilities: A-

A high Facilities grade indicates that the campus is aesthetically pleasing and well-maintained; facilities are state-of-the-art, and libraries are exceptional. Other determining factors include the quality of both athletic and student centers and an abundance of things to do on campus.

Campus Dining

The Lowdown On...
Campus Dining

Freshman Meal Plan Requirement?

Yes (included in room and board fees)

Meal Plan Average Cost:

Meal plan charges are included in overall campus housing costs. Non-residents can purchase a meal plan for $1,116–$1,160 per semester.

Places to Grab a Bite with Your Meal Plan:

Residential Dining Halls and Cafés:

You can purchase meals at the following places using your meal plan.

Bruin Café

Food: Coffee, pastries, sandwiches
Location: Sproul Hall

→

(Bruin Café, continued)

Hours: Monday–Thursday
7 a.m.–12 a.m.,
Friday 7 a.m.–2 a.m.,
Sunday 7 p.m.–2 a.m.

Covel Commons Residential Restaurant

Food: Pizza, pasta

Location: Covel Commons

Hours: Monday–Friday
11 a.m.–9 a.m.,
5 p.m.–9 p.m., Saturday–
Sunday 11:30 a.m.–3 p.m.,
5 p.m.–9 p.m.

Crossroads Café

Food: Mexican

Location: Tom Bradley
International Hall

Hours: Sunday–Thursday
9 p.m.–12 a.m.

**De Neve
Residential Restaurant**

Food: Sandwiches, entrees

Location: De Neve Plaza

Hours: Monday–Friday
7 a.m.–10 a.m., 11 a.m.–2 p.m.,
5 p.m.–8 p.m., Saturday–
Sunday 9:30 a.m.–2 p.m.,
5 p.m.–8 p.m.

**Hedrick Residential
Restaurant**

Food: Asian, sushi, salad

Location: Hedrick Hall

Hours: Monday–Thursday
(11 a.m.–2 p.m., 5 p.m.–8 p.m.,

(Hedrick, continued)

Sunday 10:30 a.m.–2 p.m.,
5 p.m.–8 p.m.

Puzzles Café

Food: Burgers, hot dogs, pizza,
breakfast

Location: Sunset Village

Hours: Monday–Thursday
9 a.m.–11 a.m., 8 p.m.–2 a.m.,
Saturday 7 p.m.–2 a.m.

Rieber Residential Restaurant

Food: American, international

Location: Rieber Hall

Hours: Monday–Friday
7 a.m.–9 a.m., 11 a.m.–2 p.m.,
5 p.m.–8 p.m., Saturday–
Sunday 11:30 a.m.–3 p.m.,
5 p.m.–8 p.m.

On-Campus Restaurants:

The following are restaurants
located on campus. You can't
purchase food here with your
meal plan, but you can pick
up some student coupons for
a discount.

Bombshelter

Food: Pacific Rice & Noodle
Traders, Grab & Go Gourmet,
Kikka Sushi, Roadside Grill,
Stacks Deli, Rosarita Grill

Location: Court of Sciences

Hours: Monday–Thursday
7:30 a.m.–3:30 p.m.,
Friday 7:30 a.m.–3 p.m.

Café Synapse

Food: Pasta, pizza, sandwiches, specialty drinks

Location: Gonda Center

Hours: Monday–Thursday
7:30 a.m.–5 p.m.,
Friday 7:30 a.m.–4:30 p.m.

Cooperage ("the Coop")

Food: Taco Bell, Shorty's
Subs, Krispy Kreme, Athena's,
Roadside Grill

Location: Ackerman Union

Hours: Monday–Thursday
7:30 a.m.–9:30 p.m.,
Friday 7:30 a.m.–9 p.m.

Espresso Roma Café

Food: Sandwiches, salads

Location: Anderson School
of Business

Hours: Monday–Thursday
7 a.m.–9 p.m.,
Friday 7 a.m.–7 p.m.,
Saturday 9 a.m.–5 p.m.,
Sunday 10 a.m.–7 a.m.

Kerckhoff Coffee House

Food: Baskin Robbins, Grab
& Go Gourmet, Kikka Sushi,
Good For You (vegetarian)

Location: Kerckhoff Hall

Hours: Monday–Thursday
7 a.m.–11 p.m.,
Friday 7 a.m.–7 p.m., Saturday–
Sunday 8 a.m.–6 p.m.

LuValle Commons

Food: Pacific Rice & Noodle
Traders, Roadside Grill,

(LuValle Commons, continued)

Honorable Subs, California
Toss (pizza and salad)

Location: Near School of Law

Hours: Monday–Thursday
7:30 a.m.–9 p.m.,
Friday 7:30 a.m.–4 p.m.,
Saturday 11 a.m.–3 p.m.

North Campus Student Center

Food: Stacks Deli, Casa Norte
(Mexican), California Café
(pizza, entrees), Burger Express,
Grab & Go Gourmet

Location: Near Young
Research Library

Hours: Monday–Friday
7 a.m.–7:30 p.m.

Northern Lights

Food: Baskin Robbins, Kikka
Sushi, coffee, pastries

Location: North of Rolfe Hall

Hours: Monday–Friday
7 a.m.–7:30 p.m.

Terrace Food Court

Food: Tropix (smoothies,
wraps), La Cucina by Sbarro
(Italian), Panda Express
(Chinese), Colombo (frozen
yogurt), Rx (candy), Rubio's
(Mexican), Relaxation (boba,
tea), Wetzel's Pretzels

Location: Ackerman Union

Hours: Vary by restaurant, but
those that serve dinner are
open weekdays 10 a.m.–8 p.m.
and weekends 11 a.m.–5 p.m.

Tsunami

Food: Asian noodles, Kikka Sushi

Location: Ackerman Union

Hours: Monday–Thursday 10 a.m.–7:30 p.m., Friday 10 a.m.–5 p.m.

Off-Campus Places to Use Your Meal Plan:

None, but you can order pizza from Rieber until 12 a.m.

Student Favorites:

Bombshelter

Cooperage

Terrace Food Court

Did You Know?

There is a **sack-lunch program** that dorm residents can use to swap a dorm lunch for a sack lunch, which includes a sandwich, fruit pack, and chips.

Students Speak Out On...
Campus Dining

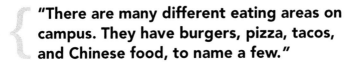

{ **"There are many different eating areas on campus. They have burgers, pizza, tacos, and Chinese food, to name a few."**

"The food is great here. In the dorms, **they pride themselves on the number of food options available**, and the dining halls are nationally-ranked as some of the best food at any university. On campus, there are a whole bunch of coffee shops, a Taco Bell Express, Rubio's, and Sbarro, just to name a few. And if you don't like any of those restaurants, you have Westwood right next door with many restaurants and Cafés."

"Food on campus is good, and there's a large variety of it. There's a Rubio's, Wetzel's Pretzels, Sbarro, Panda Express, Baskin Robbins, and Krispy Kreme Donuts. **You can basically get any type of food, and it's pretty cheap**. The dorm food is good for dorm food. There's a large variety of food in the dorms to choose from."

"**The dining halls are excellent**. They always change up the menu. On campus, there are three regular dining places plus there is a Baja Fresh and Panda Express."

"I'd say the food is pretty good compared to other college campuses. In my opinion, **Rieber dining hall is the best dining hall**, and Covel Commons is the worst."

The College Prowler Take On...
Campus Dining

Dorm dining on campus is truly hit or miss, but if you plan right you can hit big. Starting with the dorms, the best strategy is to plan ahead. The food at each dorm hall varies, and jumping from dorm to dorm is usually the best method to keeping a variety of foods in your life (check out the menu online at *www.dining.ucla.edu*) Keep eating at the same place, and the pizza and hamburgers will start to taste too familiar. You'll soon find your feast in the cereal section. Realistically, the food is nutritious and delicious if you survey the scene ahead of time. Be sure to check out the late-night places to eat for a tasty midnight snack that will pack on the pounds. Some favorites include the lasagna dish from Caruso's Deli, late-night pizza from Rieber, or the "Triple Bypass" (a chili cheese dog with fries and a large coke) from Puzzles. It's worth it to get a 14-meal-a-week plan as opposed to the 21-meal-a-week plan. This is the best for grabbing an occasional shake or late-night snack without having an excessive amount of meals left over at the end of the quarter.

Aside from the dorms, food on campus is not anything spectacular. Although there are many places to choose from, there is not any one place that has food that is overwhelmingly tasty. The taste buds kick at all of the places around campus when you're hungry. Although the campus cuisine is fulfilling, it is not good enough to write home about.

The College Prowler® Grade on

Campus Dining: A-

Our grade on Campus Dining addresses the quality of both school-owned dining halls and independent on-campus restaurants as well as the price, availability, and variety of food.

Off-Campus Dining

The Lowdown On...
Off-Campus Dining

Restaurant Prowler:
Popular Places to Eat!

Acapulco
Food: Mexican
1109 Glendon Ave.
(310) 208-3884
Cool Features: Great food specials, especially Mondays.
Price: $9 and under
Hours: Monday–Friday
11 a.m.–11 p.m.,

(Acapulco, continued)
Saturday 12 p.m.–10 p.m.,
Sunday 12 p.m.–11 p.m.

**BJ's Chicago Style
Pizza & Grill**
Food: American
939 Broxton Ave.
(310) 209-7475
www.bjsbrewhouse.com
Cool Features: Besides Chicago-style pizza, BJ's offers a large selection of sandwiches, burgers, salads, and appetizers.

➜

(BJ's, continued)
Price: $10 and under
Hours: Sunday–Thursday
11 a.m.–12 a.m., Friday–
Saturday 11 a.m.–12:30 a.m.

California Pizza Kitchen
Food: Pizza
1001 Broxton Ave.
(310) 209-9197
Food: American
Cool Features: Over 30
different types of pizza.
Price: $10 and under
Hours: Monday–Saturday
11 a.m.–10 p.m.,
Sunday 12 p.m.–9 p.m.

**Canter's Delicatessen
and Restaurant**
Food: Deli
419 N Fairfax Ave.
(323) 651-2030
www.cantersdeli.com
Cool Features: Authentic
East Coast diner on the West
Coast. Open 24 hours and
on all holidays, except Rosh
Hashanah and Yom Kippur.
Price: $10 and under
Hours: Daily 24 hours

Damon & Pythias
Food: American
1061 Broxton Ave.
(310) 824-8777
Cool Features: Healthy,
affordable, and super tasty.
Price: $12 and under

(Damon & Pythias, continued)
Hours: Monday–Saturday
11 a.m.–10 p.m.

Diddy Riese
Food: Cookies
926 Broxton Ave.
(310) 208-0448
Cool Features: You can get
four cookies for a dollar.
Price: $2 and under
Hours: Monday–Saturday
10 a.m.–6 p.m.

Enzo's Pizzeria
Food: Italian
10940 Weyburn Ave.
(310) 208-3696
Cool Features: Mafioso
atmosphere to go with your
pepperoni pizza.
Price: $8 and under
Hours: Monday–Wednesday
11 a.m.–12 a.m., Thursday–
Saturday 11 a.m.–3 a.m.

Gushi
Food: Korean Food
978 Gayley Ave.
(310) 208-4038
Cool Features: Low cost,
authentic Korean cuisine.
Price: $7 and under
Hours: Monday–Saturday
10:30 a.m.–11 p.m.

Headlines

Food: American

10922 Kinross Ave.

(310) 208-2424

Cool Features: Great food specials, especially Monday night.

Price: $9 and under

Hours: Monday–Sunday 11 a.m.–10 p.m.

In-N-Out Burger

Food: American, grille

922 Gayley Ave.

(310) 208-2821

Cool Features: Great burgers, greater price.

Price: $6 and under

Hours: Sunday–Thursday 10:30 a.m.–1 a.m., Friday–Saturday 10:30 a.m.–1:30 a.m.

Jerry's Famous Deli

Food: Deli

10925 Weyburn Ave.

(310) 208-3354

www.jerrysfamousdeli.com

Cool Features: Traditional deli food, late-night dining, and the "New York/Broadway" theme make this one of the most popular restaurants in Los Angeles.

Price: $10 and under

Hours: Daily 24 hours

Lamonica's New York Pizza

Food: Pizza

1066 Gayley Ave.

(Lamonica's, continued)

(310) 208-8671

Cool Features: Classic New York thin-crust pizza with plenty of tasty toppings to choose from.

Price: $10 and under

Hours: Daily 10:30 a.m.–12 a.m.

Mel's Drive-In Restaurant

Food: American

1650 N Highland Ave.

(323) 465-2111

www.melsdrive-in.com

Cool Features: The classic 50s-style drive-in diner featured in the movie American Graffiti.

Price: $10 and under

Hours: Daily 24 hours

Napa Valley Grill

Food: Californian

1100 Glendon Ave.

(310) 824-3322

Price: $50 and under

Hours: Monday–Thursday 11:30 a.m.–3:30 p.m., 5:30 p.m.–10:30 p.m., Friday–Saturday 11:30 a.m.–3:30 p.m., 5:30 p.m.–11 p.m., Sunday 5:30 p.m.–10 p.m.

Noodle Planet

Food: Asian noodles

1118 Westwood Blvd.

(310) 208-0777

Cool Features: A wide variety of authentic Asian noodle dishes (especially Thai).

Price: $10 and under

(Noodle Planet, continued)
Hours: Sunday–Thursday
11:30 a.m.–11 p.m., Friday–
Saturday 11:30 a.m.–1 a.m.

Sak's Teriyaki
Food: Japanese
1121 Glendon Ave.
(310) 208-2002
Price: $10 and under
Hours: Monday–Sunday
11 a.m.–9:30 p.m.

**Subbies Roll-Inn Sandwich
(AKA "Buck Fifty's")**
Food: Submarine sandwiches
954 Gayley Ave.
Cool Features: They used to
have 8-inch hoagies for $1.50
(which prompted the store's
student-given nickname, "Buck
Fifty's"). They recently had to
raise prices a bit, but you still
won't pay more than 3 bucks.
Price: $3 and under
Hours: Daily 9 a.m.–1 a.m.

Versailles
Food: Cuban
10319 Venice Blvd.
(310) 558-3168
Cool Features: Garlic
barbecue chicken.
Price: $12 and under
Hours: Sunday–Friday
11 a.m.–10 p.m.,
Saturday 11 a.m.–11 p.m.

Did You Know?

Acapulco has free buffet-style appetizers and
half-priced meals on Monday nights.

Other Places to Check Out:

Baja Fresh
California Pasta CO
Gypsy Café
Habibi Café
Le Chine Wok
Moustache Café Restaurant
Olive Garden
Shakey's Pizza
Subway
Thai House
Togo's Eatery
Westwood Brewing Company

Student Favorites:

Damon & Pythias
Gushi
Noodle Planet
Subbies Roll-Inn Sandwich

Grocery Stores:

Ralph's
10861 Le Conte Ave.
Los Angeles
(310) 824-5994

Whole Foods Market
1050 Gayley Ave.
Los Angeles
(310) 824-0858

24-Hour Dining:

Canter's Delicatessen
and Restaurant
Mel's Diner

Starving Student Food Specials:

Enzo's Pizzeria
Lamonica's New York Pizza
Noodle Planet

Best Asian Food:

Sak's Teriyaki

Best Breakfast:

Headlines

Best Healthy:

Damon & Pythias

Best Pizza:

Enzo's Pizzeria

Best Place to Take Your Parents:

Napa Valley Grill

Students Speak Out On...
Off-Campus Dining

"Westwood has a decent selection of good, cheap restaurants. In-N-Out Burger and Shakey's are my favorite commercial franchises. The Westwood Brew Company has great food and good beer."

Q "Westwood has a ton of good restaurants within walking distance of campus and the surrounding living areas. You get **everything from fancy dining to good cheap spots**. My favorites are Damon and Pythias, California Pasta Company, Jerry's Famous Deli, BJ's, and Noodle Planet."

Q "**The restaurants off campus are really diverse**. Acapulco, In 'n Out, California Pizza Kitchen, Diddy Riese, BJ's, Moustache Café and Roll In (you'll have to ask around to find Subbies Roll-Inn Sandwich) are all good places in Westwood. Plus, there are tons of little places to eat, as well."

Q "**There are many restaurants in Westwood, and most are very good**. Some of the bigger names are BJ's, Jerry's Famous Deli, Olive Garden, Baja Fresh, Subway (open 24 hours), and Togo's."

Q "There are plenty of restaurants off campus, but I haven't been to all of them. **BJ's is a nice pizza place**. There's In 'n Out burgers, Noodle Planet, Le Chine Wok, Thai House, California Pizza Kitchen, Jerry's Famous Deli, Gypsy Café, Habibi Café, and a bit more. It's all in the Westwood area, which is right outside of campus."

Q "Right outside the campus in Westwood Village is where you have all the great places. At the famous Diddy Riese, you can buy humongous cookie ice cream sandwiches, and you can pick from many different cookies. This place is crazy. They only cost one dollar, and juice or milk is only 25 cents! It's a great place. There are plenty of other places to eat. **You'll find something for your taste bud in the village.**"

Q "The food in Westwood is good, but I don't particularly like the Olive Garden. **In-N-Out's always good when you can't decide where to go.** There's also this cookie store close by called Diddy Riese's. It's only a quarter for each cookie and a dollar for an ice cream sandwich. It's a fraction of what they charge at Mrs. Fields, and they taste just as good. You'll definitely have to try it."

Q "Good spots off campus are Noodle Planet (Asian), Enzo's (Italian), Jerry's Famous Deli (**celebrities hang out here**), Sak's Teriyaki (my favorite!), and Acapulco's (Mexican)."

The College Prowler Take On...
Off-Campus Dining

An off-campus restaurant jaunt is always in order for students with a little more time and money to spend. For the lunch crowd, a quick step to Damon and Pythias will produce a healthy and incredibly delicious meal for around $10. The meals here are simply staggering, and the steak sandwich with blue cheese dressing is heavenly, and it's only $8.75. Trying a soup is a can't-miss proposition, and the soups are less at $7. Sepi's, a cheaper option, offers up a great submarine sandwich that's sure to leave an impression. Each of the subs here are named after UCLA Bruin greats such as John Wooden, Bill Walton, or Kareem Abdul-Jabbar. The price here runs about $7 per sub. The best-priced subs in town can be found at Subbies Roll Inn Sandwich; it's $2.75 for a six-inch sub. The toppings are nothing to rave about, but the prices certainly are. Roll In has been shut down twice over the last five years for health violations, but poor college students tend to overlook such things.

Los Angeles has every type of food imaginable, and most of it is close to Westwood. While at UCLA, make sure to take advantage of the plethora of food options around you. It will be an educational and culinary experience that your stomach will surely thank you for!

The College Prowler® Grade on

Off-Campus
Dining: A

A high off-campus dining grade implies that off-campus restaurants are affordable, accessible, and worth visiting. Other factors include the variety of cuisine and the availability of alternative options (vegetarian, vegan, Kosher, etc.).

Campus Housing

The Lowdown On...
Campus Housing

Undergrads Living On Campus:
35%

Number of Dormitories:
10

Number of University-Owned Apartments:
3 complexes

Best Dorms:
Rieber Hall, Saxon Suites, Sproul Hall

Worst Dorms:
Dykstra Hall, Hedrick Hall, Hilgard Houses

→

Dormitories:

De Neve Plaza

Floors: 4

Capacity: 1,462

Bathrooms: Private by room

Coed: Yes, by room

Residents: Mostly freshmen

Room Types: Doubles, triples

Special Features: Dining hall, auditorium, fitness room, computer lab, study area, laundry room

Dykstra Hall

Floors: 10

Capacity: 871

Bathrooms: Communal

Coed: Yes, by room

Residents: Mostly freshmen

Room Types: Doubles, triples

Special Features: TV lounges, laundry room

Hedrick Hall

Floors: 7

Capacity: 982

Bathrooms: Communal

Coed: Yes, by room

Residents: Mostly freshmen

Room Types: Doubles, triples

Special Features: Computer lab, study lounge, pool table, Ping-Pong table, music practice room, fitness room, dining hall

Hedrick Summit

Floors: 9

Capacity: 825

Bathrooms: Private by suite

Coed: Yes, by room/suite

Residents: Mostly upperclassmen

Room Types: Singles, doubles, triples

Special Features: Floor lounges, laundry, music practice rooms, dining hall

Hilgard Houses

Floors: 2

Capacity: 120

Bathrooms: Communal

Coed: Yes, by room

Residents: Single transfer students

Room Types: Studio apartments

Special Features: Living rooms, study areas, 24-hour computer lab, outdoor patios

Hitch Suites

Floors: 3

Capacity: 315

Bathrooms: Private by suite

Coed: Yes, by suite

Residents: Mostly upperclassmen

Room Types: Suites

Special Features: Private entry

Rieber Hall

Floors: 7

Capacity: 967

(Rieber Hall, continued)

Bathrooms: Communal

Coed: Yes, by room

Residents: Mostly freshmen

Room Types: Doubles, triples

Special Features: Computer lab, study lounge, fireside lounge, large screen TV, pool table, Ping-Pong table, conference room, music practice room, fitness room, dining hall

Rieber Vista

Floors: 9

Capacity: 623

Bathrooms: Private by suite

Coed: Yes, by room/suite

Residents: Mostly upperclassmen

Room Types: Doubles, triples, single-room suites

Special Features: Laundry, fitness rooms, computer labs, study lounges, music practice rooms, dining hall

Saxon Suites

Floors: 3

Capacity: 374

Bathrooms: Private by suite

Coed: Yes, by suite

Residents: Mostly upperclassmen

Room Types: Suites

Special Features: Private entry

Sproul Hall

Floors: 7

Capacity: 953

(Sproul Hall, continued)

Bathrooms: Communal

Coed: Yes, by room

Residents: Under- and upperclassmen

Room Types: Double, triple

Features: Computer lab, study lounge, fireside lounge, photo lab, large screen TV, pool table, Ping-Pong table, conference room, music practice room, fitness room

Sunset Village

Floors: 4

Capacity: 1,464

Bathrooms: Private by room

Coed: Yes, by room

Residents: Mostly upperclassmen

Room Types: Doubles, triples

Special Features: Laundry, dining hall, computer lab

University Apartments North

Seven complexes located west and southwest of campus

Bathrooms: Private

Coed: Yes, but apartments are single-sex

Residents: Single transfer students and upperclassmen

Room Types: Two- and three-bedroom apartments

Special Features: Laundry facilities, utilities included in rent

University Village

1,160 apartments located five miles south of campus

Bathrooms: Private

Coed: Yes

Residents: Student families

Room Types: One-, two-, and three-bedroom apartments

Special Features: State-of-the-art childcare center, community centers, computer lab, central courtyards, playground, swimming pools

Room Types:

Single, double, triple, suite

Bed Type

Extra-long twins are the staple bed for all the dorms. Bunk beds and lofts are standard for the triple rooms.

Available for Rent

A MicroFridge is $200 to rent for the year.

Cleaning Service?

Each floor in the dorms has a washer and two dryers available for $1.50 per wash and $0.75 per dry. The suites have one large room with eight washers and dryers for the students to use.

What You Get

A bed, desk, closet, phone, cable, free cable, and access to UCLA TV.

Also Available

You can borrow a hub to share the Ethernet line.

Students Speak Out On...
Campus Housing

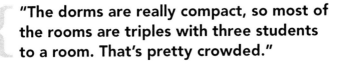

"The dorms are really compact, so most of the rooms are triples with three students to a room. That's pretty crowded."

Q "There are four high-rise dorms and three suite/apartment-style complexes. All of them **have their own dining hall, a small computer lab**, and some even have a fitness room and/or a recreation room with pool tables. I lived in Hedrick for two years and think that it had the best dining hall, Sproul is kind of blah, and Dykstra is the most social."

Q "The dorms are pretty good. Avoid Sproul Hall—its suites are the best, but are way too expensive. **The Plazas' suites are not worth the money** either."

Q "Of the three complexes, **Hitch is predominantly transfer student housing**, Sunset is supposed to be pretty nice, and De Neve is new and also supposed to be nice. The complex rooms are apartment-like or suite-style though, which makes them quieter and less social than the highrise, dorm atmosphere, where everyone's room opens into the same main hallways."

Q "Dorms are a problem. UCLA is jamming three people into doubles, and it is nearly unbearable. They just built a new housing complex called De Neve Plaza, which is pretty nice, but there is still a housing crunch. **Most kids only live in the dorms their freshman year**."

Q "Dorms are okay. I'd say avoid rooms that are close to the trash chute, as they tend to smell pretty bad. Otherwise, most of the dorms are cool. Sunset Village dorms are a little different from the rest; instead of a communal bathroom, each room has their own private bathroom. **It's kind of like your own studio apartment minus the kitchen and living room**. De Neve Plaza is our newest dorm building. I heard those are pretty nice, but I haven't been in them yet."

Q "I've really enjoyed living in the dorms. That's why I've been here so long! The dorms are really convenient because they are right next to campus. There are some dorms to avoid, but it really depends on what you're looking for. If you want the social scene, I'd recommend Dykstra or the highrises, but if you want something quieter, De Neve Plaza or Sunset Village are good choices. **If you want the apartment style life, then Hitch or Saxon are good**, although a lot of second-years go here, and they are a hike really far up a hill."

Q "**Dorms are crappy**. I don't know how I lived with three other people in one tiny, little room. I think I was in denial at the time. I'd recommend Sproul Hall or Sunset Village. The suites, Saxon and Hitch, are so much better. Try to get those with your friends during your second year if at all possible."

The College Prowler Take On...
Campus Housing

When living on-campus, students basically have two lifestyle choices: 1) live like honeybees packed into a hive, all the while making many friends and living a very social lifestyle, or 2) enjoy peace, quiet, and spacious privacy (not to mention paying a little extra). Many claim that the on-campus unity that comes along with living in the dorms offsets the horrendous conditions. To keep the conditions as pleasing as possible, try to live further down the hill. Dykstra Hall is the closest dorm, and after a day of studying, you probably don't want three staircases to climb before you get to your room. You can try Sproul Hall or Rieber, but by all means, stay away from Hedrick. It's the highest dorm on the hill, and the west side of the building is directly over the kitchen vents, which suck in the rotten smell of whatever the vents are blowing out. Now, compare that with Sproul Hall, where all the doughnuts are made fresh every night for the following breakfast and smell the dorm up with a glazed goodness.

Suites are more expensive and don't offer the same communication opportunities as the dorms do, but for some extra space, many people think that the suites are worth the money. You'll get an additional living room space which doubles as a social area, and you'll also have a semi-private bathroom. Whatever your concern, the cramped nature of the freshmen dorms is kind of a "rite of passage" into the college realm. UCLA works each year to expand the tight quarters of on-campus housing. Until then, underclassmen should just get used to the tenament-style living.

The College Prowler® Grade on

Campus Housing: C

A high Campus Housing grade indicates that dorms are clean, well-maintained, and spacious. Other determining factors include variety of dorms, proximity to classes, and social atmosphere.

Off-Campus Housing

The Lowdown On...
Off-Campus Housing

**Undergrads in
Off-Campus Housing:**
65%

Average Rent For:
Studio: $900/month
1BR Apt.: $1,200/month
2BR Apt.: $1,500/month
3BR Apt.: $2,000/month

Popular Areas:
Brentwood, Santa Monica,
Westwood

**Best Time to Look
for a Place:**
Try to secure a place before
Spring Break

For Assistance, Contact:
(800) RENT-005
info@westsiderentals.com
www.westsiderentals.com
Charge: $50 for service
Also check in the *Daily Bruin*

Students Speak Out On...
Off-Campus Housing

"Westwood Village is the closest housing to school. It's quite expensive, but students pay for the convenience of living close to campus."

Q *"**Off-campus housing is expensive**. You can find less convenient housing in nearby West LA, Palms, or south of Wilshire for a lot cheaper."*

Q *"If you look in the Daily Bruin, our school paper, you might find some people in Bel Air who are willing to provide free room and board in exchange for hours of baby-sitting or other household chores. It doesn't sound too bad, but it depends on the family. If they're super freaky, **I'd rather pay rent than live with psychos**."*

Q *"**I would say live on campus, unless you really know what you are getting into**. The fact that you have to cook every day for yourself is a big change. You can find housing off campus, but it is expensive and most likely a dump."*

Q *"I hear that off-campus housing isn't so bad. I lived in Westwood my last year, and the walk was only 20 minutes. For people who live in West LA and take the bus, I hear that it wasn't so bad either; you just have to get up earlier. **You have to start looking up to one year ahead to get housing in Westwood, though**."*

The College Prowler Take On...
Off-Campus Housing

Off-campus housing is a major change from the easy lifestyle of the dorms. Finding a place to live in Westwood is easy if you're willing to pay big bucks. However, it's worth it for some to be in the mix of apartment and frat parties, along with a minor 15- to 30-minute walk from class. Many students share rooms in Westwood just to make the living affordable. Remember that there is usually only one parking spot per room in the apartments, so if each room in the house harbors two students, parking could become very cramped. The housing prices here are steep, and for the price of a two-room, you could easily find a three-room on the outskirts of Brentwood, West Los Angeles, Santa Monica, or Palms.

Moving to a place slightly farther away from campus makes a large difference. Although many warn of the "commute" when living farther from campus, the time it takes to get to school is comparable. If you know the bus schedule, and live near a bus stop, you can get to school in the same amount of time as the people that live in Westwood. The bus is free with student ID, so living outside of Westwood is much more affordable and quiet. However, the price of living off campus and staying involved in the Bruin bubble is often too high for most students to bear, and that drops the grade on UCLA's off-campus housing.

The College Prowler® Grade on

Off-Campus Housing: B-

A high grade in Off-Campus Housing indicates that apartments are of high quality, close to campus, affordable, and easy to secure.

Diversity

The Lowdown On...
Diversity

African American:
3%

Native American:
Less than 1%

Asian American:
38%

White:
34%

Hispanic:
15%

Unknown:
5%

International:
4%

Out-of-State:
6%

Political Activity

Most of the minority groups are politically active, and at least once a year they try to raise awareness of a larger concern.

Gay Pride

There is campus resource center and major designed towards lesbian, gay, bisexual, and transgender education and awareness.

220 Kinsey Hall
(310) 206-3628
www.saonet.ucla.edu/lgbt
lgbt@ucla.edu
Monday, Tuesday, Thursday 8:30 a.m.–8 p.m.
Tuesday and Friday 8:30 a.m.–6 p.m.

Economic Status

The economic diversity here spans the spectrum. There are rich and poor students of every ethnicity, but certain groups tend to attract a rich and snobbish stereotype. Don't let stereotypes speak for the group. Many students are easygoing and approachable despite the pre-painted picture.

Minority Clubs

The minority clubs at UCLA are a political juggernaut on campus. There is a political action group at UCLA that is mainly comprised of the minority clubs and associations on campus. See the Student Organizations section for more information.

Students Speak Out On...
Diversity

> "There are all races at the campus, although the majority of the undergrad population is Asian and Caucasian."

Q "I think that the campus is very diverse. There seems to be good diversity in most departments. Coming from high school, I only hung out with people from my own race, but coming to UCLA, **I met tons of people from different backgrounds just by opening my door** in the dorms. I have a wide array of friends from Asian to Caucasian to Latino to Indian. With so many cultures, there are many opportunities to meet new people."

Q "The largest groups of students are Asians followed by Caucasians. Those two groups make up probably 80 percent of the campus. There are not many African Americans or Latinos. However, it is probably one of the most diverse campuses in the United States. There are **student groups for almost every nationality you can think of**. The drawback is that the school is pretty racially-segregated."

Q "Los Angeles is just **one huge melting pot**."

Q "**UCLA touts its diversity, despite the fact that it's very ethnically segregated**. In spite of this, UCLA's campus is truly more diverse than many others I've visited."

Q "For the most part, UCLA is a somewhat diverse campus. If you're an outsider looking at UCLA, you would see a lot of Caucasians and Asians, but once you get to meet more people, and find out about the different organizations, you find that **UCLA has a lot to offer in terms of people with different backgrounds**."

The College Prowler Take On...
Diversity

The sheer diversity on UCLA's campus can be viewed as both strikingly evident and a misnomer. Despite the falling numbers in minority enrollment over recent years, there is still a strong showing of minorities within the UCLA world. The diverse groups at UCLA do their best to welcome other members of similar races and show their pride around campus. There are ethnic clubs that give diversity some stature on campus such as the African Student Union, Mecha (for Hispanic students), and the Asian Pacific Coalition. Much racial intermingling occurs through intramural sports, parties, and interest-based clubs. Some people are intimidated by ethnic clubs and for that reason stray away from embracing other cultures. The vocalization of the minority groups makes minorities seem more plentiful on campus. Take a look at the percentages and note how the numbers are higher for some minorities than they are for others.

Despite the shortcomings, UCLA's campus is one of the most diverse in the United States. Minority students on campus also have many resource centers and readily interact with the rest of the campus through exhibitions and culture shows that occur each week. On a personal level, making a friend for life with a person of another race is easily possible. You will definitely see diversity everywhere on campus.

The College Prowler® Grade on

Diversity: A+

A high grade in Diversity indicates that ethnic minorities and international students have a notable presence on campus and that students of different economic backgrounds, religious beliefs, and sexual preferences are well-represented.

Guys & Girls

The Lowdown On...
Guys & Girls

Male Undergrads:
45%

Female Undergrads:
55%

Birth Control Available?

Yes, visit Arthur Ashe Student Health and Wellness Center, 221 Westwood Plaza. Open Monday, Wednesday, and Friday 8 a.m.–6:30 p.m.

Social Scene

There is a great amount of social interaction within the separate majors and minority groups at UCLA. Generally, people inside of classes are very helpful and talkative. Intermingling with people outside of a major is a little more difficult. But this is where living in the dorms can be such a resource, as people exchange ideas and phone numbers all the time.

Hookups or Relationships?

There are many students always looking to hook up, and at the same time there are many students that are in committed relationships. Due to the size of the campus, there is no real way to know or categorize. However, one general rule states that students tend to look for relationships more as they get older.

Best Place to Meet Guys/Girls

Due to the weather at UCLA, you will hardly ever see heavy coats obstructing the awesome bodies of the majority of the students. Most students are not afraid to let it all hang out either. Bruin Walk and the surrounding areas are usually filled with students of all shapes and sizes. Also, students tend to use Bruin Walk as a thoroughfare to class. So, spotting a hottie while you are walking to class is also a distinct possibility.

The bar scene is also busy almost every night. Here, you'll most likely find the sorority and fraternity crowd. Don't be fooled by the matching Tiffany's bracelets, these girls are different, and talking to them will unlock their charm and wit. The same goes for the guys, but their personalities take a more fluid state as the drinks go down, so try to catch them before they've had one or two too many.

Did You Know?

Top Three Places to Find Hotties:

1. Maloney's
2. Bruin Walk
3. Powell Library basement

Top Five Places to Hook Up:

1. Frats
2. Private study rooms in the Young Research Library
3. Powell Library basement
4. Sculpture Garden
5. Treetop

Dress Code

The main difference between Southern California style and the rest of the world is that it is decidedly more casual. T-shirts, shorts, and sandals are mandatory if the weather is over 75 degrees. A designer sweater is all that's needed if the cold hits, and anyone wearing more than that is calling attention to themselves. The UCLA community is accepting of other types of dress. After all, the atmosphere is, again, casual.

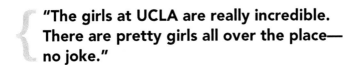

"The girls at UCLA are really incredible. There are pretty girls all over the place— no joke."

Q "There are more girls at UCLA than guys—maybe that's because girls are smarter! In my opinion, the girls are hotter than the guys, and they're in really good shape, too. Everyone here seems to be really fit, I guess that's a So-Cal thing. **You see a lot of gym-obsessed, eating-disorder types, too**."

Q "If you're a South Campus major, **everyone there is pretty nerdy and unattractive**."

Q "The guys and girls here are, for the most part, stereotypically LA. They are overly concerned with style, appearance, and whatnot. I'd say that there are a lot of hot chicks, but **relatively few attractive guys**."

Q "**There are some pretty good-looking guys and girls at UCLA**. There is no shortage of eye candy! Although the guys may be hot, they are pretty arrogant. The girls are really pretty but kind of catty and snobby. UCLA is really influenced by Hollywood."

Q "Hot guys and girls? Yep, I'd say so. See, **UCLA is a part of the Los Angeles scene**, and being right next to Westwood (a pretty high-class city), the students tend to be materialistic and up-to-date with fashion."

Q "**It's amazing how many hot women are on North Campus in the fall and spring**. I'm a South Campus major, and we never really get any of the hotties down here. I guess humanities is a chick magnet of its own at UCLA. I'm not kidding when I say that women make school here enjoyable and that I wish I had majored in art."

Q "It depends where you look, but there are many good-looking guys here. In my experience, all the good ones are either taken or like your brothers, but I have tons of friends who met significant others here easily. It depends on what your focus is, though. I have found that **when I go clubbing or to the bars, everyone is good looking**."

Q "**UCLA has many attractive people with a lot to offer any prospective suitor**. There are many different types of people with different interests, and everyone will find someone for them on campus."

The College Prowler Take On...
Guys & Girls

Despite having a reputation for cookie-cutter men and women, UCLA is a very diverse campus when it comes to its guys and gals. Students at UCLA are beautiful and intelligent, this goes for all the departments. If you are looking, which many UCLA students are, you are sure to find whatever type of physical attraction that suits your taste. The eclectic backgrounds of the students provide a variety of distinct looks. The Greek system, on the average, usually consists of people that look similar in dress and they tend to be superficial, but despite the stereotype, many participants of the Greek system are delightfully social and try individualize themselves as much as possible.

Being in Southern California certainly boosts UCLA's grades for hotness. Instead of having to wait until spring, skin is shown year-round due to Los Angeles' beautiful weather. The students are very friendly, for the most part, and you'll get to know the ones in your selected major particularly well. Students here shouldn't be afraid to talk to a hot guy or girl, no matter what they look like—most students want to get to know a variety of different people. When it comes to congeniality and devastating looks, the bar is set pretty high at UCLA.

The College Prowler® Grade on

Guys: A-

A high grade for Guys indicates that the male population on campus is attractive, smart, friendly, and engaging, and that the school has a decent ratio of guys to girls.

The College Prowler® Grade on

Girls: A

A high grade for Girls not only implies that the women on campus are attractive, smart, friendly, and engaging, but also that there is a fair ratio of girls to guys.

Athletics

The Lowdown On...
Athletics

Athletic Division:
Division I

Conference:
Pac 10 (Pacific)

School Mascot:
Bruin

Colors:
Scarlet and white

**Men Playing
Varsity Sports:**
319 (3%)

**Women Playing
Varsity Sports:**
304 (2%)

→

Men's Varsity Sports:

Baseball
Basketball
Cross country
Football
Golf
Soccer
Tennis
Track and field
Volleyball
Water polo

Women's Varsity Sports:

Basketball
Cross country
Golf
Gymnastics
Rowing
Soccer
Softball
Swimming & diving
Tennis
Track & field
Volleyball
Water polo

Club Sports:

Archery
Badminton
Baseball
Bowling
Crew
Cycling
Equestrian
Fencing
Field hockey
Gymnastics
Ice hockey
Kayak polo
Kendo
Lacrosse
Roller hockey
Rugby
Running
Sailing
Skiing/snowboarding
Soccer (women's only)
Surfing
Table tennis
Taekwondo
Triathlon
Ultimate Frisbee
Volleyball
Water polo
Water skiing/wakeboarding
Weight training
Wrestling

Intramurals:

Alpine skiing
Badminton
Basketball
Bowling
Cricket
Cycling
Dodgeball
Flag football
Golf
Handball
Racquetball

(Intramurals, continued)

Sailing
Soccer
Softball
Squash
Swimming
Table tennis
Tennis
Track and field
Volleyball
Water polo

Athletic Fields

Rose Bowl, Intramural Field, and Drake Stadium

Getting Tickets

Tickets are best purchased before the season starts. If you're a big sports fan, you should snatch up a Bruin season-ticket package. Student packages are cheaper than face-value tickets and will seat you in the student section with all of the other rowdy sports fans. If you don't grab up one of these packages, prepare yourself for long lines to buy tickets for a sporting event.

Most Popular Sports

Men's basketball season is always sure to bring about two things: 1) high expectations, and 2) a jam-packed Pauley Pavilion. Reserve your seats early. Football is also a popular sport, but the majority of the fun happens before the game at the tailgate parties.

Overlooked Teams

The women's softball team is constantly winning championships without much of anyone noticing. The same goes for men and women's track teams, whom are always competitive and rarely receive publicity.

Best Place to Take a Walk

The sculpture garden is serene, yet small. Also, check out the Japanese Gardens in Bel Air.

Gyms/Facilities

John Wooden Center

The John R. Wooden Center is a newly-remodeled athletic center with workout facilities, a gym for basketball and intramural sports, racquetball courts, a rock-climbing wall, and a program book full of extra-curricular classes and activities. The weight room gets crowded daily from 12 p.m. until 3 p.m., and the basketball courts usually jam up from around 6 p.m. until 9 p.m., and on Friday starting at 2 p.m. until 6 p.m.

Men's Gym

This gym harbors many of the best games of pickup basketball in the UCLA area, especially in the summer when the pros come out to play.

Students Speak Out On...
Athletics

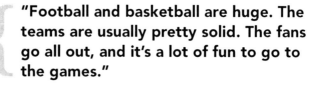

"Football and basketball are huge. The teams are usually pretty solid. The fans go all out, and it's a lot of fun to go to the games."

Q **"Basketball and football are the only two college sports that get any serious attention at UCLA**. Intramural (IM) sports don't seem to be that huge, but they are around."

Q **"The sports program is thriving**, although many students never pay attention to them. I've heard that IM sports are also popular."

Q "Both varsity and intramurals are huge. I have never participated in IM sports, but there are ample opportunities to participate if you like that. We have a huge sports program, and men's football and basketball are huge. **I think a lot of funding goes to sports, and going to games is definitely an experience in itself**."

Q "Sports are very big; especially football and basketball, as we always field a good team. **The IM sports get lots of attention, as well**. Sometimes they feature competitive teams with really talented players."

Q "UCLA has lots of school spirit; it's actually really fun if you get into it. However, UCLA basketball hasn't been doing so well the last couple of years, but that hasn't really affected the school spirit. As long as you're interested in them, **IM sports are as big as any other UCLA sport**. There are IM sports for pretty much any and all sports."

Q "Basketball tickets are kind of hard to get. You have to **order season tickets in advance**. IM sports are not that big. There is a large variety of sports, but I don't really know many people who have participated in them."

The College Prowler Take On...
Athletics

Varsity sports are what initially put UCLA on the map. There's a reason that *Sports Illustrated* named UCLA their "jock school of the century." In retrospect, it seems like every year a national title is won in at least one of the many varsity sports. The strength of the two most popular sports, men's basketball and football, sets the tone for the rest of the year, especially in the dorms and fraternities. Men's basketball has the storied lore of Wooden to attain each year, as Pac 10 championships are always demanded. You can feel the anticipation in the air when fall rolls around, as the football team usually steamrolls the early season competition and sets up hope for another long-awaited national title run. Attending the games indulges the student in the frenzied action, and the ticket availability fluctuates with the success of the team. Because of the vast number of things to do in LA, people tend to tune out the major sports if they don't do so well. If the basketball team is winning, you'd better hope that you bought season tickets; the student section tickets will be more impossible to get your hands on than a nearby parking spot.

The sheer joy of having a successful sports program brings out the gym rats in all shapes and forms. IM sports have different levels of competition, usually separated into three levels. Athletics at UCLA are larger than life, and they make the student experience that much better.

The College Prowler® Grade on

Athletics: A-

A high grade in Athletics indicates that students have school spirit, that sports programs are respected, that games are well-attended, and that intramurals are a prominent part of student life.

Nightlife

The Lowdown On...
Nightlife

Club and Bar Prowler:
Popular Nightlife Spots!

Circus Disco

6655 Santa Monica Blvd.
Hollywood

(323) 462-1291

This place is a gold mine of musical talent, especially on Saturday nights with Spundae. The world-class DJs keep the place on its feet, and it has been nominated for best dance

(Circus Disco, continued)

club in Los Angeles. There are multiple rooms, so the music changes from location to location. The thundering bass and electronic vibes will surely keep your legs pumping and swaying all the way home. Parking is $5 outside of the club.

Friday: House, Electronic, Latin, Hip-Hop; $10 Cover

Saturday: Flava; House, R&B, Latin, Hip-Hop; $10 Cover

Sunday: Spundae; House and Trance; $25 Cover

The Ivar

6356 Hollywood Blvd.
Hollywood

(323) 465-4827

www.ivar.com

The Ivar is located in the heart of Hollywood, and is one block west of the world's most famous intersection, Hollywood and Vine. The architecture is spellbinding, and the club is enormous, with enough space to fit 1,500 people. Club goers beware; there is usually a stiflingly long line outside if you arrive past 10:30 p.m.

Thursday: Fidelity; electronic, techno; $20 cover

Friday: Kitsch; hip-hop, R&B, electronic; $20 cover

Saturday: Engine driver; hip-hop, R&B, electronic; $20 cover

Maloney's on Campus

1000 Gayley Ave.
Westwood

(310) 208-1942

This bar houses the most TVs in all of Westwood, and is an absolute madhouse whenever there is a sporting event. Student sports-fans, and those older ones that can't let go of their college roots, will find Maloney's the place to be for any sporting occasion.

Miyagi's

8225 West Sunset Blvd.
Los Angeles

(323) 650-3524

(Miyagi's, continued)

Miyagi's has succulent sushi that will make your wallet burst into flames from the inflated price. Many students don't come here for the sushi, however. The secret to Miyagi's is to be inside the restaurant after 10 p.m. Once the dance floor emerges on the third floor, swallow down the sushi, if you've splurged, and lead your date out to boogie down.

Nightly: hip-hop, no cover

Tengu

10853 Lindbrook Dr.
Los Angeles

(310) 209-0071

Named after a group of elusive long-nosed goblins in Japanese folklore, Tengu is a very hot Asian-fusion restaurant, as well as a great bar. Sundays are half-price sake nights. No cover.

W Bar

930 Hilgard Ave., W Hotel
Los Angeles

(310) 208-8765

This bar offers a modern, chic alternative to the loud, and student-saturated, local bar scene. Set in the amazing W Hotel, a first class building of its own, the ambiance of the bar is more New York than UCLA. The velvet ropes may be intimidating, but the intimacy inside of the bar is stunning, especially on the weekdays. For a date that's slightly out of the

(W Bar, continued)

ordinary, check out this swanky yet subtle jewel tucked away on the outskirts of Westwood.

Westwood Brewing Company

1097 Glendon Ave.
Westwood

(310) 209-2739

Skip the bottlenecks in favor of one of their handcrafted ales, a Westwood Blonde or Pear Cider. This is the only microbrewery in Westwood, so enjoy the variety here. Happy hour is from 3 p.m. to 7 p.m., $2.50 beers and half-price appetizers. Sundays from 11 a.m. to 3 p.m. come to watch some football with $2 pints and Bloody Mary's, and buffalo wings at 25 cents each. There's live entertainment every night All shows start at 9 p.m., and you must be 21. No cover.

White Lotus

1743 Cahuenga Blvd.
Hollywood

(323) 463-0060

This posh bar houses celebrities nightly and only the swankiest can cross the velvet ropes of this club. Access is limited, so get there early and get ready to pay the $5 parking fee. If your group is up to it, the VIP parking upgrade for $20 may be even better for easier access to and from the club.

Wednesday–Saturday: Hip-Hop and R&B, $20 cover

Other Places to Check Out:

Hollywood Canteen

The Saddle Ranch

The Sunset Room

Student Favorites:

Maloney's

Westwood Brew Company

Tengu

Cheapest Place to Get a Drink:

Maloney's

Local Specialties:

Microbrews from Westwood Brewing Company

Primary Areas with Nightlife:

West Hollywood (20 minutes)

Sunset Strip (15 minutes)

Santa Monica (10 minutes)

Melrose (10 minutes)

Bars Close At:

2 a.m., there are some after-hours bars in Hollywood/Downtown that close at 9 a.m.

Favorite Drinking Games:

Beer Pong

Card Games

Century Club

Quarters

Power Hour

Useful Resources for Nightlife:

www.la2nite.com

www.groovetickets.com

www.source7.net

What to Do if You're Not 21

The Cow's End

34 Washington Blvd., Marina Del Rey
(310) 574-1080

There are plenty of comfy couches and delicious smoothies here to melt away the daily stress while you curl up with a good book. The local crowd is relaxed and on certain nights there are live performances. The Cow's End also houses a computer with Internet connection for some quick e-mail check ups, and plug-ins. Beware the loud writers talking to studio heads about their prospective manuscripts. While amusing, these people are extraordinarily loud in the otherwise tranquil atmosphere.

The Grand Avenue Night Club

1024 S. Grand Ave., Downtown LA
(213) 747-0999

Grand Avenue Night Club is one of downtown LA's premiere club venues. The balcony is a cool place to chill and get your drink on with another full bar in the middle. The club is modern and definitely large in scale. There are plenty of students from all over Los Angeles at this club.

Wednesday: "Wet Wednesday" $20 cover; electronic

Thursday: "Downtown Live" $12 cover; Hip Hop, Latin, rock/pop

Saturday: "Club Union" $15 cover; Hip Hop/ R&B, reggae/world

Students Speak Out On...
Nightlife

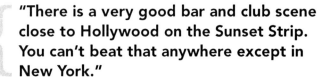

"There is a very good bar and club scene close to Hollywood on the Sunset Strip. You can't beat that anywhere except in New York."

Q "UCLA is fairly close to Hollywood and the Sunset Strip where **you'll find all of the famous clubs and bars**, so I don't think you'll have a problem finding one. The trouble is finding one that you like. It's all preference. As long as you drive yourself, or know someone who can drive you, there won't be any trouble finding either of these two places."

Q "Westwood Brew Company is my favorite place; it has a great social scene. The Sunset Strip is a 10-minute drive away and has a bunch of great clubs, restaurants, and bars. **The social scene is awesome**!"

Q "**For clubs, it depends on what kind of music you like**. It is LA, so you'll find at least one that you like, trust me!"

Q "**Don't go to bars and clubs near campus**. This is one of the biggest cities in the country! You really won't have a shortage of spots, so be adventurous."

Q "Just look up Sunset Strip on the Internet and **you'll get an idea of how crazy it is**. There are two local bars in Westwood that are pretty good. Some nights are 18-and-over."

Q "First of all, there is no club scene in the village, thanks to our rich old neighbors who have forgotten that they live in a college town. **The homeowner's association banned clubs, but we do have some bars**. We have three bars in Westwood. They are good, but the best of all is the Westwood Brewery Company. They make their own great beers. Most students go to West Hollywood to the Sunset Strip. It gets really crazy there; traffic is a nightmare on the two-mile stretch of bars and clubs. It's a famous place; you'll see celebrities, lots of young people, and rich kids driving Vipers. After all, Beverly Hills and the rich and famous are only one block away."

Q "One place to go to is Hollywood. Santa Monica also has clubs. Unfortunately, this isn't New York where clubs and bars close around 3:30 a.m. And being in L.A., you need a car to go to these places, even though they seem close. Yes it's true, traffic is horrible here and **at night you don't want to catch a bus, especially in Hollywood**; it's not safe to be alone there."

Q "We're in LA, so there's a ton of clubs. They're further away from campus though, so you'd need to take a taxi or get a ride. **There are a whole bunch of bars and clubs on the Sunset Strip, where many celebrities hang out** like Miyagi's and the Saddle Ranch. The Sunset Room and the Hollywood Canteen are also great places; celebrities hang out there, too!"

The College Prowler Take On...
Nightlife

Nightlife in and around UCLA can be hit-or-miss. Campus parties tend to be on the milder side, and dorm parties definitely make a high school-gym party look stellar in comparison. Don't expect to find much happening in the dorms because of the strict alcohol and noise policies. The closest parties near campus usually go down at the fraternity houses, and the fraternity members are somewhat exclusive about their guest lists (chicks with tight skirts and see-through clothing need not worry). Men may want to look into frequenting the local bar scene at Maloney's, or checking out some of the neighborhood apartment parties. Maloney's is packed for every Lakers and UCLA game. For those with a car and the desire to branch outside of Westwood, the options are promising. There are many clubs on Sunset Strip or further down in Hollywood worth stopping by. For a different feel, there are also clubs in the downtown area that harbor a more intense energy and Santa Monica definitely provides a more relaxed environment.

For those who aren't 21, nightlife can be difficult to engage in. If you don't have a car, then life becomes bound to the Westwood bubble. Without a vehicle (or a friend that has a vehicle), it's difficult to fully indulge in LA's nightlife. If you do, however, the Sunset Strip is only 15 minutes away, and there are after-hours bars open until 10 a.m..

The College Prowler® Grade on

Nightlife: A-

A high grade in Nightlife indicates that there are many bars and clubs in the area that are easily accessible and affordable. Other determining factors include the number of options for the under-21 crowd and the prevalence of house parties.

Greek Life

The Lowdown On...
Greek Life

Number of Fraternities:
19

Number of Sororities:
11

Undergrad Men in Fraternities:
13%

Undergrad Women in Sororities:
13%

→

Fraternities:

Alpha Epsilon Pi
Alpha Tau Omega
Beta Chi Theta
Beta Theta Pi
Delta Sigma Phi
Delta Tau Delta
Phi Kappa Pi
Pi Kappa Alpha
Pi Kappa Phi
Sigma Alpha Epsilon
Sigma Chi
Sigma Nu
Sigma Phi Epsilon
Sigma Pi
Theta Chi
Theta Xi
Triangle
Zeta Beta Tau
Zeta Psi

(For more info on each of these organizations check out: *www.bruinifc.com*)

Sororities:

Alpha Delta Pi
Alpha Epsilon Pi
Alpha Phi
Chi Omega
Delta Delta Delta
Delta Gamma
Gamma Phi Beta
Kappa Alpha Theta
Kappa Delta
Kappa Kappa Gamma
Pi Beta Phi

(For more info on each of these organizations check out *www.studentgroups.ucla.edu/panhellenic*)

Other Greek Organizations:

Greek Council
Greek Peer Advisors
Interfraternity Council
Kappa Zeta Phi
Lambda Phi Epsilon
Omega and Sigma Tau
Order of Omega
Panhellenic Council
Theta Kappa Phi

Students Speak Out On...
Greek Life

"Greek life at UCLA fits the stereotype like one of those round little pegs. Sadly enough, it does sort of dominate the social scene."

Q "It's not for everybody, but it is definitely something to consider if you're interested. As far as the social scene, the **big party night at UCLA is Thursday**, and usually there are at least two or three parties in the fraternities going on."

Q "It's active, but by no means necessary. **Why bother going Greek if you have LA at your fingertips**?"

Q "I think that UCLA is very racially segregated, so basically all of the white kids join the Greek system in an attempt to form their own group. I found the Greek system to be really obnoxious mainly because it was so **segregated and geared towards white students**. Once people enter the Greek system, they seem to only associate with each other."

Q "The Greek system does not dominate the social scene at all. There are so many other events going on, you sometimes have a hard time choosing which to attend. **There are several wonderful clubs to join**. If you have a hobby, there's probably a club for it."

Q "Frat parties are on Thursday nights, but I haven't experienced it because it just doesn't seem like my scene. But if you enjoy **hanging out with people who drink socially**, the Greek system just might be your place here."

"Numerous fraternities and sororities exist at UCLA, including special-interest (i.e. business and community service oriented) and coed ones. Joining a Greek organization can be a great way to make close friends with common interests, and attend fun social activities. If you don't join a fraternity or sorority, that doesn't mean that you can't have a social life. In fact, you can still attend their parties and functions, depending on the event. But not being a member also means that you may not be able to experience to the **close bond of brotherhood or sisterhood that the chapter shares**. Greek life may not be for everyone, but you won't know until you check it out."

The College Prowler Take On...
Greek Life

Greek life at UCLA is utilized by many active members as a center for sharpening social skills and giving back to the community. The Greek party scene is definitely worth checking out (if you can get in) and some of the shenanigans that occur at the Greek houses resemble those that you see on TV or at the movies. Both sororities and fraternities have "exchanges," or date parties, once or twice a week. For much of UCLA's student population, especially first-year students, the vein into the Greek body seems like the only way to become socially active and stop watching from the sidelines. As overwhelming as it may seem at times, the Greek system does not dominate the social scene. Many students find solace at the local bars, and for those that can drive, on the Sunset Strip and in Santa Monica.

Being Greek at UCLA is really all in how one perceives it. If you talk to a frat brother, he might tell you that the hazing that he went through was all part of a bonding experience meant to bring together 18 pledges with butt-paddling delight. Talk to a sorority sister and she will tell you that the sheer ecstasy of being treated like a diva-queen for a quarter or two is well worth the process of being chosen. If you're in a Greek organization, you will definitely have access to your fill of fun each week as they hold open parties each week that are sure to draw masses and masses of wild and crazy Bruins.

The College Prowler® Grade on
Greek Life: B

A high grade in Greek Life indicates that sororities and fraternities are not only present, but also active on campus. Other determining factors include the variety of houses available and the respect the Greek community receives from the rest of the campus.

Drug Scene

The Lowdown On...
Drug Scene

Most Prevalent Drugs on Campus:
Acid
Alcohol
Ecstasy
Marijuana

Alcohol-Related Referrals:
605

Alcohol-Related Arrests:
6

Drug-Related Referrals:
64

Drug-Related Arrests:
18

Drug Counseling Programs

Arthur Ashe Student Health and Wellness Center
221 Westwood Plaza

The Arthur Ashe Student Health & Wellness Center's Health Education Unit is one of many campus departments that work in a partnership with student groups to empower the majority who want to promote a healthy and safe campus environment around the issues of alcohol and other drug abuse. For additional information, call the Health Education Center at (310) 825-6385.

Students who are struggling with symptoms related to personal or someone else's alcohol or drug use might call the Student Psychological Services (SPS) at (310) 825-0168.

Students Speak Out On...
Drug Scene

> "I know a guy who knows a guy. Seems like that is the way it is on this campus—everyone knows, but nobody does it."

 "The drug scene is not so obvious, but I think **everyone smokes pot**. I think it's another story if you're in the school of Arts and Architecture, though. I hear the students and professors enjoy doing a ton of drugs."

Q "Drugs are thriving. In all seriousness, **I feel that drugs are just as popular here as they are anywhere else**. I would say there are plenty of pot smokers, and coke and ecstasy users. I wouldn't say that it dominates the University life, though."

Q "**At least 20 people a day are smoking marijuana on campus that I know of**, and on April 20 (4/20), there are hundreds of people smoking on campus. Weed is very visible and accessible, but the harder drugs are a little more hidden in their use."

Q "**Weed is popular and readily available**. Some kids do harder stuff, and some kids would never touch a joint. There's a large variety."

Q "Stoners unite. **April 20 (4/20) is a big deal on campus**, and there are a lot of people who do ecstasy and other party drugs. You'll see every drug imaginable depending on who you choose to spend time with. I wouldn't advise using, but if you do, at least remember that you should do so in moderation."

Q "**College is a time for experimentation**, so it depends on the crowd you end up with. However, it's no secret that you can get marijuana and some other drugs pretty easily if you know where to go."

The College Prowler Take On...
Drug Scene

Just because drugs are not always out in the open at UCLA does not mean that they do not exist. Many daring pot smokers won't hesitate to light up and smoke on any area of campus. UCLA is by no means a "druggie" school. You won't normally see people smoking as you walk from class to class, nor will you smell the scent of marijuana, but if students want to smoke, it is there. The only day that there is noticeable drug usage on campus is on April 20 (the infamous 4/20) when hundreds of students openly light up on campus in a festive manner. Other than 4/20, though, on-campus drug usage is minimal, probably because of the large presence of the UC Police Department and student officers that peruse the campus.

Off-campus drug usage is common for students that want to explore the medium. Marijuana is the most available drug followed by ecstasy, then cocaine. Most students do not plunge further into the realm of drug usage than that, and classes require more attention than the daily use of drugs allows. Oh yeah, UCLA students tend to consume alcohol from time to time.

The College Prowler® Grade on
Drug Scene: C

A high grade in the Drug Scene indicates that drugs are not a noticeable part of campus life; drug use is not visible, and no pressure to use them seems to exist.

Campus Strictness

The Lowdown On...
Campus Strictness

What Are You Most Likely to Get Caught Doing on Campus?
- Drinking underage
- Parking illegally
- Making too much noise in your dorm
- Downloading copyrighted materials
- Skateboarding
- Stealing food from the dorms
- Having candles and incense sticks in your dorm
- Running stop signs
- Not showing your ID when you enter the dorm

Students Speak Out On...
Campus Strictness

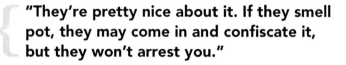

"They're pretty nice about it. If they smell pot, they may come in and confiscate it, but they won't arrest you."

Q "I've heard about people getting busted for pot in the dorms, and I think **you get put on academic probation** for that. You just have to be careful."

Q "I've never met anyone who has had a problem with the police for **breaking minor policies**."

Q "In the resident halls, there is a no-tolerance policy for drugs. If you're caught with marijuana, not only will you be cited, but **you will also loose your financial aid** (if you're on it). As far as drinking, there is a closed-door policy in the dorms. You can drink so long as you are not breaking any other rules or regulations of on-campus housing—no more than two guests per resident present when alcohol is in the room, and no bulk alcohol. If there is a lot of noise in the room, or if complaints are being filed and there is drinking going on in the room, you will be cited."

Q "They aren't too strict in regards to alcohol. **The campus is supposed to be dry**, but they don't raid or anything. Just keep the doors closed. They do get involved when it becomes a disturbance."

Q "In my experiences with the campus police and security guards, I have typically found them to be extremely strict when compared with other schools that my friends attend. Security really seems to be ever-present. They are always around, and **they are equipped with magic noses**."

Q "On-campus drugs and **drinking policies are very strict and are no joke**—they mean what they say: absolutely no exceptions. I learned this the hard way. Before classes had even begun my freshman year, I had already lost my on-campus housing privileges. One afternoon, I had decided to smoke a few joints in a dorm with a friend that I had met at orientation. We thought that we had gotten away with it; about an hour later, however, we were sitting there in his room, chilling, listening to music, when a knock came at the door. The RAs said they smelled marijuana coming from the room. They took a look around and found no hard evidence that we were smoking pot, aside from the smell. Two weeks later, both he and I were asked to leave campus housing. If you want to keep your housing, then there are plenty of opportunities to party off campus."

Q "UCLA is located in a very rich neighborhood, and **where there is a lot of wealth, you'll find a lot of law enforcement**. Just take a look at our rival USC and compare the neighborhoods. Students do drink in their dorms, but it's social, not stupid drinking. The only drug you'll ever see, and that I have ever seen, is marijuana."

Q "Although frats give out alcohol, I don't think the school actually condones it. It does happen, though, and I think that every once in a while, if the drinking becomes excessive, there'll be police involved. Otherwise, nothing really happens. As far as drugs go, I don't know. I don't tend to smell pot unless it's 4/20, but it happens. If they don't catch you, they won't know who's doing what. But I **don't really see any drugs going around**."

Q "Here's what our resident director says: 'Just don't let me hear and see it.' Of course, **don't be stupid and carry an open alcoholic beverage in public**."

Q "It's a dry campus, but the police don't seem to be too strict. **I've never had a problem**, and I've never heard of anyone having a run-in with the police over drugs or drinking."

Q "**They bust people for smoking pot up at the dorms**, but most every stoner I've ever met hasn't been caught. Drinking is allowed in your dorm room if you have the door shut."

Q "If they catch you with alcohol in the dorms and you are a minor, you can get in big trouble, but **it all depends on your resident advisor (RA)**."

The College Prowler Take On...
Campus Strictness

UCLA claims to support a zero-tolerance policy. But many students claim that this is not entirely the truth. While there are many policemen and student officers cruising around campus, there is not much animosity toward them. Rather, the officers are often more than willing to assist students with any problems that may occur. Since there are rarely any major problems on campus, the officers tend to leave students alone. This does not mean that cops won't do their jobs, though. These officers will not hesitate to write a citation on the spot, so be cautious and know that the consequences are only a citation away.

Currently, security is much more lax in the dorms than in years past. Many resident assistants (RAs) are students themselves and they want to make your college experience enjoyable. The rules are enforced, but not in a way that is overwhelming or intimidating. Even students who get caught drinking won't find the repercussions too harsh. In fact, drinking is permitted in the dorms as long as the door is closed. Enforcers of the rules at UCLA make a point of not being overbearing. From time to time, complaints arise about cops busting people for seemingly inconsequential reasons such as skateboarding or disorderly conduct. Most of the time, though, there is a reason that students are apprehended, and the police understand that this is a college town, and many times will let bygones be bygones.

The College Prowler® Grade on

Campus
Strictness: C+

A high Campus Strictness grade implies an overall lenient atmosphere; police and RAs are fairly tolerant, and the administration's rules are flexible.

Parking

The Lowdown On...
Parking

Approximate Parking Permit Cost:
$72–$327 per quarter

Parking Services:
555 Westwood Plaza
Los Angeles
(310) 794-RIDE
www.parking.ucla.edu

Student Parking Lot?
There are several student and faculty lots around campus.

Freshmen Allowed to Park?
Yes

Common Parking Tickets:
Expired Meter: $38
No Stopping Zone: $62
Handicapped Zone: $500
Fire Lane: $62
Parking with Invalid Permit: $42

Parking Permits

You must apply for a permit by the fifth week of the preceding quarter. This deadline is strictly enforced. Parking permits are granted on a points system. Your points vary depending on your distance from school, whether or not you have a job, if you are going to carpool, and how far away your job is from campus.

Did You Know?

Best Places to Find a Parking Spot

In the evenings, park down on Westholme Drive, in the morning and early afternoon, metered parking on North Campus and in Lot 6 are your best bets, but a long shot at that. You're better off buying parking at Lot 32 and riding the shuttle directly into campus.

Good Luck Getting a Parking Spot Here!

You will never find paid day parking on campus after 8 a.m.

Students Speak Out On...
Parking

"Many people who apply for parking do not get it. It's a point-based system, and it's very hard to understand it, let alone conquer it."

Q "Parking is horrendously hard to get. Don't expect to be able to get on-campus parking in any of the UCLA lots. Street parking is also very restricted and hard to find in the entire Westwood area, and the non-UCLA lots in Westwood that you can get monthly overnight parking in are outrageously expensive. **Only bring a car if you are really going to need it frequently**."

Q "**Parking is not easy**. Street parking is terrible, meter parking is terrible, and permit parking is terrible. If you want a permit, get it extremely early. Otherwise, you can ride the bus."

Q "Parking sucks. If you're looking to get a permit to park, that's probably not going to happen, as there is a lot of construction going on to make a new parking lot. But until then, there is a **huge shortage of parking**. If you have friends coming to visit, they can purchase one-day parking passes, or if they come after 9 p.m. and leave before 7 a.m., they can park at the meters for free. Otherwise, metered parking is 25 cents per eight minutes! That kind of sucks. I don't like parking here."

Q "Parking on campus is a pain. If you live in the dorms, it's **most likely that you will not get a parking permit on campus**, which means you will have to buy it off someone, or park somewhere off campus."

Q "It is hard to find a parking spot off campus, and there's a two hour limit from 9 a.m. to 6 p.m. on most of the streets, so you have to move your car often. **The meters on campus are a total rip-off**. I wouldn't recommend having a car while living in the dorms unless you have a parking permit, or can buy a space off someone."

Q "Good luck getting parking. They raised daily parking rates to over seven dollars a day! **Avoid commuting to school**, if possible. However, the Big Blue Bus is free for UCLA students with the swipe of a Bruin Card."

The College Prowler Take On...
Parking

At UCLA, parking can only be garnered if you apply by week six of the previous quarter, and even then, there are no guarantees. The passes are awarded via a point system based on questions such as how far you live and work from campus. The only problem is that it seems like everyone lies on the forms. Apparently it is possible to live in central California while working in San Diego and still attend UCLA. Knowing these facts, good luck trying to get a parking pass. If you can't get parking, do yourself a favor and park your car down the road and cruise in on the Big Blue Bus, at least it's free!

Parking is extremely difficult here. If you're commuting from off campus, try for the big points in the questionnaire like carpooling. Anyone can buy a night parking pass, which is good everyday after 4 p.m. and all weekend for $90. Even still, the fact that a student cannot find parking at his or her own school is a major disgrace. Especially when you consider that the paid parking on campus is $7, and after 8 a.m., you have to park in the lot off campus. Parking on campus is limited to two hours at the meters, and good luck trying to find a meter at any time during the day. UCLA also loses major points for starting the free parking time on campus at 9 p.m. Unfortunately, these free spaces are only effective for extracurricular activities. Really, what did you expect from a school in Los Angeles?

The College Prowler® Grade on

Parking: F

A high grade in this section indicates that parking is both available and affordable, and that parking enforcement isn't overly severe.

Transportation

The Lowdown On...
Transportation

Ways to Get Around Town:

On Campus
Fleet & Transit Services:
(310) 206-2908
Hours: Monday–Friday
7 a.m.–7 p.m.

UCLA Campus Van Service:
(310) 825-1491
Hours: Monday– Thursday
6 p.m.–12 a.m.

Public Transportation
Santa Monica Big Blue Bus
(310) 451-5444
www.bigbluebus.com/home/index.asp
Fare: $0.75 Full, Students ride free with their Bruin Card
Hours: Monday–Friday
8 a.m.–5 p.m.

➡

(Public Transportation, continued)

Culver City Bus Lines
(310) 253-6500
*www.culvercity.org/
depts_bus.html*
Fare: $0.75 Full, $0.50 Student
Hours: Monday–Friday
8 a.m.–5 p.m.

Los Angeles Metropolitan
Transit Authority
(800) COMMUTE
www.mta.net
Fare: $1.35

Taxi Cabs

Bell Cab
(888) 235-5222

Yellow Cab Co.
(800) 200-0011

United Independent Taxi
(800) 822-8294

Car Rentals

Alamo
Local: (310) 937-9611
National: (800) 327-9633
www.alamo.com

Avis
Local: (310) 646-5600
National: (800) 831-2847
www.avis.com

Budget
Local: (310) 474-9948
National: (800) 527-0700
www.budget.com

(Car Rentals, continued)

Enterprise
Local: (310) 649-5400
National: (800) 736-8222
www.enterprise.com

Hertz
Local: (310) 568-3400
National: (800) 654-3131
www.hertz.com

National
Local: (310) 388-8200
National: (800) 227-7368
www.nationalcar.com

Thrifty
Local: (310) 475-7341
National: (800) 847-4389
www.thrifty.com

Best Ways to Get Around Town

Hitch a ride from a friend

Big Blue Bus—with student ID, the fare is only $0.25

Rollerblade from point A to point B

Ways to Get Out of Town:

Airport

Los Angeles
International Airport
(310) 646-5252

The Los Angeles International Airport is 10 miles and approximately 30-minutes driving time from UCLA

Airlines Serving LAX

American Airlines
(800) 433-7300
www.americanairlines.com

Continental
(800) 523-3273
www.continental.com

Delta
(800) 221-1212
www.delta-air.com

Northwest
(800) 225-2525
www.nwa.com

Southwest
(800) 435-9792
www.southwest.com

TWA
(800) 221-2000
www.twa.com

United
(800) 241-6522
www.united.com

US Airways
(800) 428-4322
www.usairways.com

How to Get There

First, head out onto Wilshire Blvd. Then, merge directly onto I-405 South. Stay on I-405 until you see the LAX Airport exit. Take the ramp toward Century BL West/LAX Airport, then turn left onto La Cienega Boulevard.

A cab ride to the airport costs around $35.

Amtrak

800 N. Alameda St.
Los Angeles
www.amtrak.com

The Amtrak station is in downtown Los Angeles.

Greyhound

1715 N. Cahuenga Blvd.
Los Angeles
www.greyhound.com

Travel Agents

Archer Travel
(818) 248-1511

STA Travel
(310) 824-1574

Students Speak Out On...
Transportation

> "The Big Blue Bus and Culver City Bus are your best bets. They'll get you almost anywhere you'd need to go if you can't afford to have a car."

Q "We have the Big Blue Bus, **which is free to UCLA students with their ID**. That can take you to Santa Monica and Beverly Hills. I've never really used public transportation, but for more information go to *www.bigbluebus.com.*"

Q "I have the say this **public transportation is very good**. The school has a deal with the Santa Monica Bus line so that students can ride without paying."

Q "The bus system is pretty bad. **It takes forever**! Bruins can ride for free on the Santa Monica Big Blue Buses. The metro doesn't go out to the West Side. My suggestion is to make friends with someone with a car!"

Q "As long as you're able to walk to the bus stop in Westwood, **bus transportation is easy**. Calling taxis is easy as well, if that's your preference. LAX (LA International Airport) is not far from campus, but in traffic, it sometimes takes an hour to get to."

Q "The Santa Monica Big Blue Bus system is really **good and convenient for getting around West LA**, and it's free with your student card. If you want to go anywhere in other areas of LA, however, the public transportation (MTA bus system) is horrible."

Q "Traffic is insane in LA. Try to avoid peak traffic hours, and **avoid taking the 405 Freeway**. If you want to take the Redline, our little subway, it's doable. There are pamphlets on bus routes and times in the Parking Services office. If you want to go to Santa Monica, use the Big Blue Bus. It's free for students except during summer, but even then, I think the charge is less than what others pay."

Q "Bus drivers are really nice in Los Angeles. I don't mind taking the bus to school. And a little know fact that people use is driving from their house and parking closer to campus, then taking the bus to school from only a block away. Just **make sure to check the signs so that you don't get a ticket**. Street sweeping can cost a student a quality meal if they're not careful and don't pay attention."

Q "**Public transportation is actually very quick**. As UCLA students, we get free transportation with the Santa Monica Bus Line, and the LA bus Line—MTA fare is only $1.35."

Q "It's pretty convenient. **UCLA has its own shuttle system** that gets you to anywhere you want to go on, or near, UCLA quickly and without hassle."

Q "Despite what others will say, **LA has a fairly comprehensive transportation system**. Unfortunately, many MTA buses have 30-minute lag times, but they'll still get you anywhere in LA.

The College Prowler Take On...
Transportation

The one thing that makes off-campus living affordable and convenient is the Bruin Go! Program. The program allows all UCLA students free rides on any Santa Monica bus. These buses circuit throughout the neighborhoods close to UCLA and touch the beach at select points. For certain commuters, the buses are more affordable than buying parking and paying for gas each day. In fact, the serenity of not having to drive into LA traffic warrants a periodic ride on the bus.

Speaking of Los Angeles traffic, there is a reason that the traffic here is considered the worst in the nation. People refer to the freeways as "parking lots" during rush hour, and there is substantial traffic in the city practically every hour of the day. Regardless, checking out the sights without a car is unheard of for two reasons. One, the buses are irregular, and very slow. Many buses do not run by a schedule and pick up their passengers by traversing the crowded areas, and the bus lines are traffic-filled. The other problem is that there are many patches of bad neighborhoods in Los Angeles. To get to some of the famous, "touristy" parts of the city, you'll have to brave these areas. Overall, you'll need a car to truly explore Los Angeles. As far as Westwood is concerned, most students are happy with the events that happen within walking distance.

The College Prowler® Grade on

Transportation: C-

A high grade for Transportation indicates that campus buses, public buses, cabs, and rental cars are readily-available and affordable. Other determining factors include proximity to an airport and the necessity of transportation.

Weather

The Lowdown On...
Weather

Average Temperature:

Fall:	64°F
Winter:	55°F
Spring:	63°F
Summer:	71°F

Average Precipitation:

Fall:	0.7 in.
Winter:	3.1 in.
Spring:	1.4 in.
Summer:	0.2 in.

Students Speak Out On...
Weather

"The weather is usually really nice. There's always a rainy season, but usually the weather is in the 70s. On cool days, it's in the mid-60s."

"I personally hate it. **All you get here is sun, sun, and sun**. I love rain, overcast skies, and the cold. It's generally in the 70s here. In July and August, it can get into the 90s and, yes, even the 100s, but that's only in the summer, and it come in waves. Yes, it does rain, and when it rains, it's crazy. Have you heard of all the mudslides in Malibu? Well, UCLA is not that far from there. Here, rain can range from a sprinkle to very heavy. We get most of our rain in February. In the winter, it can get to as low as 30 degrees in the valley and 35 degrees in the city. Usually, the low is 45 degrees at UCLA, but it can get cold. The valley, which is right behind the mountains from UCLA, can range from 30 to 110 degrees. You come over to the city side and it's between 50 and 78. The valley is part of the city; just LA gets divided in two by the Santa Monica Mountains. But now you know why everybody loves LA; it's the weather."

"It's sunny Southern California! **We don't really have seasons**. The coldest it gets is in the 50s. Because I've lived in L.A. my whole life, I say it's freezing when it's in the 50s, but it's not all that cold. Beaches are nearby also, but if you want to go to a beach where you actually can swim safely, don't go to Santa Monica."

Q "One word describes the weather: beautiful. There's no weather like LA anywhere except the Mediterranean. It's usually sunny and clear. We do not get much rain. **That keeps the ladies in the skimpy clothing**, if you know what I mean."

Q "The weather is generally warm. It doesn't rain often. Sometimes there is morning fog, but it burns off fast. I have not needed more than a thick sweater in the winter. **It is a bit smoggy, though**. That can be bothersome."

The College Prowler Take On...
Weather

Welcome to sunny Southern California! Legend has it that Hollywood moved here for the proximity of the deserts, mountains, and perennial sunshine that makes almost every day of the year feel like summertime. The temperature stays above 55 degrees year-round. Bring a sweater for the cool winter nights, but nothing too heavy or you'll overheat. And definitely bring some rain gear for the spring showers; they last from about mid-February until the end of March. But, for the most part, load your closet with shorts or skirts because when the heat turns up, you'll definitely want to take it off!

The weather in Los Angeles is definitely a key selling point of the city. People wear T-shirts and shorts year-round, and the only time that you may need to wear any type of layering is during those winter nights where the temperature can contrast with the sunny days and drop to about 45 degrees. That is as cold as the weather will drop in Los Angeles, and some students will miss the cold weather and the skiing. Luckily, snow is only a two-hour drive from campus to nearby Big Bear Mountain. Where else in the world can you hit the beach and the ski slopes in the same day?

The College Prowler® Grade on
Weather: A

A high Weather grade designates that temperatures are mild and rarely reach extremes, that the campus tends to be sunny rather than rainy, and that weather is fairly consistent rather than unpredictable.

Report Card Summary

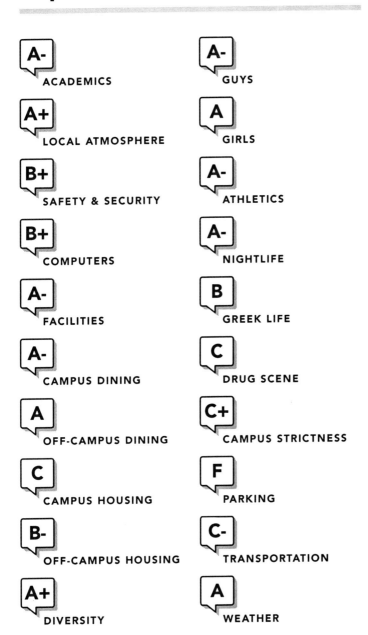

A- ACADEMICS	**A-** GUYS
A+ LOCAL ATMOSPHERE	**A** GIRLS
B+ SAFETY & SECURITY	**A-** ATHLETICS
B+ COMPUTERS	**A-** NIGHTLIFE
A- FACILITIES	**B** GREEK LIFE
A- CAMPUS DINING	**C** DRUG SCENE
A OFF-CAMPUS DINING	**C+** CAMPUS STRICTNESS
C CAMPUS HOUSING	**F** PARKING
B- OFF-CAMPUS HOUSING	**C-** TRANSPORTATION
A+ DIVERSITY	**A** WEATHER

Overall Experience

Students Speak Out On...
Overall Experience

> "I love it here. I like the people, the atmosphere, and being so close to the ocean. I like that there is so much to do. I was really unsure about the move to LA, but now I'm thinking of staying here."

Q "It's the best choice I've made. **It was my dream to come here.**"

Q "Well, I've just graduated. I'd say it was okay. **UCLA is just so darn big, and it's hard to be involved**, or really feel like you're actually a part of a school that has over 35,000 people."

Q "UCLA was a great school for me. I had a lot of fun. **There are a lot of opportunities available, so take advantage of them**. I was afraid it would be too large and impersonal for me, but I found that the opposite was true. You get a great education for the price of a state school."

Q "I definitely do not regret my choice when it comes to college. I have had nothing but good experiences here and would not trade it for the world. And I know that this sounds like a 'sell,' but honestly, I really think that if you're looking for nice people, a surrounding area full of experiences and fun, and a good academic experience, then come to UCLA. **These have definitely been the best years of my life**."

Q "At UCLA, you really are just a number. It's huge. Every day, you'll be surrounded by people you have never seen before. The key is to find a niche. You will meet so many different types of people who will really open your mind. You'll have to fight with the administration a lot, and they don't always give you help or advice. You also have to fight to get your questions answered. It's a hard school both socially and academically. UCLA had made me socially and politically aware. I guess I could say I have been hardened. **Sometimes, I wished I went to a small private school** where everyone knows your name and they hold your hand, but UCLA prepares you for the real world. Although it wasn't always smooth sailing, I wouldn't have gone anywhere else."

UCLA is a school for people who want to focus mainly on education and still have an occasional night out. There is a reason that UCLA is not a party school; the classes are too difficult to slack off for any prolonged stretch of time. However, being set amidst a Greek system that thrives on throwing boisterous parties and in close proximity to a plethora of dive bars and easygoing nightlife, staying inside all the time is nearly impossible. Add all of the campus events, speakers, workshops, and free shows to the mix, and you have something of interest for everyone in the spectrum.

UCLA challenges the students in many distinct arenas. Academically, students need to be prepared to focus on their classes beginning the first day of school. Classes demand that students study every night. Socially, students are pressed to find a niche amongst a throng of 35,000 students. Student actions tend to feel minuscule in such a large student body. Fortunately, classmates are generally polite and helpful. The first year you make friends helps scale down the exorbitant number of students of the campus and form friendships that endure the college experience. The academic and social challenge that students face is enhanced because there is no school-sponsored programs outside of the dorms that bring students together. On the brighter side, this forces many students to branch out and develop social skills that they would never have learned under the guidance of such programs. Through all of its challenges, UCLA is the ideal school to come to if you want to grow into a stronger person (physically, mentally, intellectually, socially) as students are sure to learn more than just what's inside the textbooks.

The Inside Scoop

The Lowdown On...
The Inside Scoop

UCLA Slang:

Know the slang, know the school! Absolutely everything is abbreviated at UCLA. The following is a list to help you catch on quicker:

Black Sunday – The Sunday before fall rush where the frats allow everyone in for free and it seems like a campus-wide party.

Bruin Bargains – The weekly student swap meet that occurs via the newspaper.

Bruin Walk – The central walkway that separates North Campus and South Campus.

Buck Fifty – A student nickname for Subbies Roll-Inn.

Cluster – A group of classes that, when taken together, credit the student for multiple general education classes in different subject areas (e.g. humanities, social sciences), and sometimes shave off extra classes to take.

➡

The Dungeon – A nickname for the basement area of Powell Library (one of the quietest areas to study on campus).

Fowler – The name of the classroom under the Fowler Museum.

Men's Gym – The name of the gym across from Wooden.

Midnight Yell – Finals week tradition of screaming loudly one time to relieve stress at midnight.

North Campus Majors – A nickname for social science and humanities majors because most of these departments are located on the northern half of campus.

Rape Trail – The daunting name of the (now) well-lit walkway between the dorms and the apartments.

South Campus Majors – A nickname for life and physical science majors because most of these departments are located on the southern half of campus.

Wooden – Short for the John Wooden Center.

Things I Wish I Knew Before Coming to UCLA

- Get the 14 Premier Meal Plan. It has the perfect amount of meals and extras.
- Go to the frats during Orientation Week.
- Go to the frats during Black Sunday.
- Someone in the dorms will have a microwave (and it's best if it's not you).
- Get your own bed linens.
- Your grades will plummet if you party more than you study.
- Weekends should be used for getting away to local wilderness areas.
- Visit the Career Center often to avoid being unemployed directly out of college.
- Some of the teachers are more interesting than the subjects they teach.

Tips to Succeed at UCLA

- Pick classes you actually like.
- Research your professors before choosing your classes.
- Actually go to class.
- Don't ever fall behind.
- Check your e-mail frequently.
- Ask the TAs tons of questions.
- Always dispute bad grades.
- Appear interested (even if you're not).
- Go to office hours.
- Study with other people in the class.
- Drink lots of coffee!

UCLA Urban Legends

The Inverted Fountain was designed by a USC grad that made the fountain look like a toilet when looking at the fountain with Franz Hall in the background.

School Spirit

Students are proud to be accepted into UCLA. Most freshmen are thrilled to make it into UCLA, and they carry their excitement and expectations of the school with them throughout their first year. Almost all freshman students own a UCLA T-shirt before the first day of class. The dorms light up as the sports teams charge into the national spotlight. Although the basketball and football teams don't always win the championship, students still gush about the lore UCLA carries with it. Most students engage in sporting events either by actually going to the games, or watching with friends at Maloney's. If the big game against USC ever comes up, be ready for some real student spirit to spill. The Beat 'SC Bonfire is a several thousand student event that even captivates the local media.

Traditions

Book Reading Marathon

This little jewel is an English lover's delight, as the Undergraduate English Association sponsors a reading of a book in 15-minute increments. Many times actors will come out to read the first hour of the book and support the English department.

Farmer's Market

Each Thursday, there is a large gathering of farmers that sell their produce (wholesale) on campus. Up until a few years ago, there were no grocery stores close to campus (this has changed with Ralph's and Whole Foods moving into Westwood). Most students still keep up the tradition and buy strictly from the farmers. While the prices are not always an incredible bargain, the quality is out of this world. It's worth a quick walk down to the market to indulge in some lore from the past and some quality from the present.

Inverted Fountain

All UCLA students are only supposed to touch the fountain twice in their entire UCLA career. The first time will occur during orientation, and the second will pass on the jubilant day of graduation (assuming you remember). The fountain ushers all students into the University and bids them adieu as well. It is a time-honored tradition that links all UCLA alumni.

Spring Sing

This Student Alumni Association sponsored event is a gala of the best talent that UCLA has to offer. Most students spend months preparing for this four-hour spectacle in late May. Four celebrity judges review the contestants, and there is one major music prize given to a top celebrity musician each year. Some of the past celebrity judges of the past include "Weird Al" Yankovich and Fred Savage. Some of the past musical prizewinners include Tom Petty and Frank Sinatra.

Finding a Job or Internship

The Lowdown On...
Finding a Job or Internship

Advice

Jobs are plentiful in the Los Angeles basin, but securing one is always tricky. The on-campus jobs do not pay the best amount of money, but for students with a work-study program in their financial aid that waives federal taxes, campus jobs are lucrative options. For other students, especially those with cars or knowledge of the local bus system, BruinTRAK is a good way to snag a local job or internship.

BruinTRAK is a superb vehicle for finding a job. You should call each company after you submit your resume to speak with a representative and ensure that your resume was received. Make yourself stand out by attaching a cover letter and calling the following day. Make yourself heard, and your chances of securing an interview will rise.

Career Center Resources & Services

Campus employment

Career counseling

Placement advising

Computer skills workshops

Professionalism workshops

Career resource center

Graduate school advising

BruinTRAK (daily job listings)

BruinVIEW (career resume postings and interview scheduling)

Alumni

The Lowdown On...
Alumni

Office:

UCLA Alumni Association

James West Alumni Center
Los Angeles

(800) UCLAlumni (825-8526)
(310) 825-8678 (fax)

alumni@UCLAlumni.net

www.UCLAlumni.net

The James West Alumni Center
is right between Ackerman
Union and Pauley Pavilion

Services Available:

Lifetime e-mail forwarding,
your own alumni account for
$19.99 a month, discounts on
campus events (such as gym
membership, Melnitz movies),
and discounts to local theme
parks and movie theaters.

The center's help desk can
provide you with information
about upcoming events,
membership benefits, and
membership into the student
alumni association.

Major Alumni Events

The alumni have a student run organization that holds the Beat 'SC bonfire before the big game against USC, Dinner with Twelve Strangers, which is a dinner mixing people from different majors and backgrounds for dinner with an unnamed professor, and Spring Sing which is a campus wide talent show with celebrity judges. There are also a host of career opportunities that can be explored through the SAA Career Network.

Alumni Publications

UCLAlumni magazine releases multiple issues each year free with membership.

Did You Know?

Famous UCLA Alumni:

Kareem Abdul-Jabbar – Legendary basketball player

Troy Aikman – Star NFL quarterback

Lloyd Bridges – Actor and father of actor Jeff Bridges

Nancy Cartwright – The voice of Bart Simpson

Jimmy Connors – World tennis champion

Francis Ford Coppola – Filmmaker; director of the *Godfather* trilogy

James Dean – '50s actor, and star of *Rebel Without a Cause*

Karch Kiraly – Professional volleyball player; three-time Olympic gold medalist

Jim Morrison – Rock idol; frontman for the Doors

Darren Star – Creator of *Sex In the City*, *Melrose Place*, and *Beverly Hills 90210*

Student Organizations

This is a sample list of the organizations offered at UCLA. For a complete list, as well as full explanations of what each club below has to offer and contact information, please go to the Web site *www.studentgroups.ucla.edu* and input the name of the club you are looking for in the search engine.

ACLU

Activist Librarians and Educators

Actuarial Club

Advancing Careers in Engineering and Science

Aesthetic Dentistry Study Club

Afghan Student Association

African American Studies Student Association

African-Americans in Communication, Media, and Entertainment

AFT Local 1990

Agape Christian Fellowship

AIDS Awareness Committee

Al-Anon

All Nations Christian Fellowship

Alternative Thought

Alumni Scholars Club

American Institute of Astronautics and Aeronautics (AIAA)

Amateur Radio Club

American Constitution Society

American Indian Graduate Student Association

American Institute of Chemical Engineers (AICHE)

American Library Association Student Organization

American Medical Student Association (AMSA)

American Society of Civil Engineers (ASCE)

American Society of Mechanical Engineers

American Student Dental Association ASDA

Amnesty International

Animal Welfare Association

Animation Students Organization

Armenian Students Association

Art Group

ASHA-Los Angeles

Asian American Christian Fellowship

Associated Secular Students

Astrobiology Society

Attic Dwelling Delegates (A.D.D.) for a New United Youth

Aviation Club

Awaken A Cappella

Babel Study Group for Translation Studies

Back of the Bus

Badminton Club

Bahai Association

Ballroom Dance Club and International Folk Dance Club

Barrio Youth Alternative (BaYA)

Beach & Environmental Conservation Organization (B.E.C.O.)

Beaux Arts Society

BeCarded

Best Buddies

Bhangra Team

Bharatiyam

Bicycle Advocacy Committee

Big Brothers and Big Sisters

Biomedical Engineering Society

Blood Drive Committee (SWC)

Brazilian Jiu-Jitsu Society

Bridge Club

The Brothers Grimm

Bruin Battalion

Bruin Casino Gaming Society

Bruin Democrats

Bruin Republicans

Bruin Swing Dance Club

Buddhist Value Creation Society

Business Entertainment Network: A Student Affiliation of F.A.M.E.

Business Ethics Club

Campus Bound-College Ready

Campus Crusade for Christ

Campus Editors and Writers

Campuses Organized and United for Good Health (COUGH)

CARE Council

Care Extender Internship Program

Celtic Colloquium

Chess Club

Children's Festival Club

Chinese Cultural Dance Club

Chinese Students and Scholars Association (CSSA)

Chinese Students Association

Choral Activities Support Team (CAST)

Christian Science Organization

Circle K International

CITYLAB UCLA

Classical Society

Club Capoeira Brazil

Club Medical

College Bowl Club

Collegiate Athletes Coalition

Community Outreach for Prevention and Education

Concerned Asian Pacific-Islander Students for Action (CAPSA)

Coptic Orthodox Christian Club

CPR/SFA Committee (SWC)

Critical Planning Journal

Crossroads of Language, Interaction, and Culture

Cycling Team

Dance Marathon (UCLADM)

Democratic Law Students Association

Design Student Group

Disabled Student Union

Divine Youth Associates

Earth And Space Sciences Student Organization

English Medieval Symposium

Enigma – The UCLA Fantasy and Gaming Group

Entertainment Law Association

Environmental Coalition

Episcopal Student Group

Ethiopian Student Union

Ethnographies Working Group

Evergreen – Abiding in Christ

Extensions Journal/Dance and New Media Group

FAST Club (Fashion and Student Trends)

Federalist Society

Federation Tutoring

Fellowship in Christ, Los Angeles (FICLA)

Folklore Society

Free Flow: Urban Culture Club

GAMMA (Greeks Advocating Mature Management of Alcohol)

Geography Club

Golden Key International Honor Society

Habitat for Humanity

Hare Krishna Student Organization

Health for Humanity

Health, Nutrition and Fitness Committee (SWC)

Helping Hands

Hindi Film Dance Team

Hong Kong Student Society

Hunger Project

Incarcerated Youth Tutorial Project

Indian Student Union

Indigenous Peoples' Journal of Law, Culture, and Resistance

Indonesian Bruin Student Association

Institute of Electrical and Electronics Engineers

Inter-Christian Council

International Law Society

International Peace Coalition

International Socialist Organization

Jain Bruins

Japanese Animation Club

Japanese Students Association

Jewish Student Union

Juggling Club

Justice For All: Students for Bio-ethical Equality

Korean Student Association

Latin American Student Association

Latter-Day Saint Student Association

Los Angeles Church of Christ On Campus

Marplot Poets

Math and Physical Science Council

Model United Nations

Muslim Student Association

NAACP

The Navigators

Neuroscience Undergraduate Society (NUS)

NORML

Pacific Islands Students Association

Pilipino Recruitment and Enrichment Program

Political Science Student Organization (PSSO)

Pre-Dental Society

Progressive Responses to Fashion

Project GOAL (Go Out and Learn)

Project Literacy UCLA

Psychology Society

Public Health Student Association

Queer Alliance

Race, Ethnicity & Immigration Working Group

Rally Committee

Republican Leadership Council

Sailing Team

Senior Citizen Outreach

Shakespeare Reading and Performance Group

Shooting Club

Sikh Student Association

Special Olympics

SPICMACAY (Society for the Promotion of Indian Classical Music and Culture Among Youth)

Spirit Squad

Stroke Force

Student Animal Legal Defense Fund

The Best
& Worst

The Ten **BEST** Things About UCLA

1	Decent dorm food
2	Movie premieres
3	Close proximity to the beaches
4	60 degree winters
5	Great college feel
6	Seeing actors on campus
7	Making friends of diverse races
8	The quarter system
9	Midnight food runs at the dorms
10	The architecture on campus

The Ten **WORST** Things About UCLA

1 No parking!

2 Traffic

3 Smog

4 Dirty local beaches

5 Stupid school politics

6 Student body size

7 High priced Westwood apartments

8 The need for a car to go out at night

9 Smart professors that can't speak English

10 Always under construction

Visiting

The Lowdown On...
Visiting

Hotel Information:

Best Western Royal Palace Inn and Suites
2528 S. Sepulveda Blvd.
Westwood
(310) 477-9066
Distance from Campus:
Less than one mile
Price: $99–$119

Hilgard House Hotel and Suites
927 Hilgard Ave.
Westwood

(Hilgard House, continued)
(310) 208-3945
Distance from Campus:
Less than one mile
Price: $119–$130

Hotel California
1670 Ocean Ave.
Santa Monica
(310) 393-2363
Distance from Campus:
7 miles
Price: $179–$279

➡

**Loews Santa Monica
Beach Hotel**

1700 Ocean Ave.
Santa Monica

(310) 458-6700

Distance from Campus:
7 miles

Price: $260–$349

Royal Palace – Westwood

1052 Tiverton Ave.
Westwood

(310) 208-6677

Distance from Campus:
Less than one mile

Price: $89–$120

Shutters on the Beach Hotel

1 Pico Blvd.
Santa Monica

(310) 458-0030

Distance from Campus:
7 miles

Price: $395–$595

The Standard Hotel

8300 W. Sunset Blvd.
Hollywood

(323) 650-9090

Distance from Campus:
6 miles

Price: $150–$225

W Hotel Westwood

930 Hilgard Ave.
Westwood

(310) 208-8765

Distance from Campus:
Less than one mile

Price: $260–$400

Take a Campus Virtual Tour

Visit *www.admissions.ucla.edu/tours.htm* to see photographs, a panoramic view, and a virtual tour of campus.

Take a Campus Tour

For individual reservations, visit *www.admissions.ucla.edu/ Prospect/tours.htm*.

The Housing Office offers tours of its on-campus housing facilities Monday–Friday at 12:30 p.m. Reservations are required. E-mail hao@ha.ucla.edu, or call (310) 825-4271.

The Medical Center provides tours of its facilities to interested parties. Call (310) 825-6002.

To Schedule a Group Information Session or Interview

UCLA does not schedule interviews for prospective students. However, if you would like to receive information on admission or other aspects of the University, visit the UCLA Undergraduate Admissions Office at 1147 Murphy Hall from 9 a.m. –5 p.m. or call (310) 825-3101.

Directions to Campus

Driving from the North

- Take the 405 Freeway Southbound toward San Diego.
- Take the Wilshire Blvd. East exit toward UCLA.
- Turn left onto Westwood Blvd. about a half-mile up the road.
- Once you cross La Conte another half mile up you have entered UCLA.

Driving from the South

- Take the 405 Freeway Northbound toward Sacramento.
- Take the Wilshire Blvd. East exit toward Westwood/UCLA (the first exit on the left).
- Merge onto Wilshire Blvd. and get into the left lane.
- Turn left onto Westwood Blvd. about a half-mile up the road.
- Once you cross La Conte another half mile up you have entered UCLA.

Driving from the East

- Take the I-10 Westbound toward Santa Monica.
- Merge onto the 405 Freeway Northbound toward Sacramento.
- Take the Wilshire Blvd. East exit toward Westwood/UCLA (the first exit on the left).
- Merge onto Wilshire Blvd. and get into the left lane.
- Turn left onto Westwood Blvd. about a half-mile up the road.
- Once you cross La Conte another half mile up you have entered UCLA.

Driving from the West

- Take the I-10 Eastbound toward Los Angeles.
- Merge onto the 405 Freeway Northbound toward Sacramento.
- Take the Wilshire Blvd. East exit toward Westwood/UCLA (the first exit on the left).
- Merge onto Wilshire Blvd. and get into the left lane.
- Turn left onto Westwood Blvd. about a half-mile up the road.
- Once you cross La Conte another half mile up you have entered UCLA.

Words to Know

Academic Probation – A suspension imposed on a student if he or she fails to keep up with the school's minimum academic requirements. Those unable to improve their grades after receiving this warning can face dismissal.

Beer Pong/Beirut – A drinking game involving cups of beer arranged in a pyramid shape on each side of a table. The goal is to get a ping pong ball into one of the opponent's cups by throwing the ball or hitting it with a paddle. If the ball lands in a cup, the opponent is required to drink the beer.

Bid – An invitation from a fraternity or sorority to 'pledge' (join) that specific house.

Blue-Light Phone – Brightly-colored phone posts with a blue light bulb on top. These phones exist for security purposes and are located at various outside locations around most campuses. In an emergency, a student can pick up one of these phones (free of charge) to connect with campus police or a security escort.

Campus Police – Police who are specifically assigned to a given institution. Campus police are typically not regular city officers; they are employed by the university in a full-time capacity.

Club Sports – A level of sports that falls somewhere between varsity and intramural. If a student is unable to commit to a varsity team but has a lot of passion for athletics, a club sport could be a better, less intense option. Even less demanding, intramural (IM) sports often involve no traveling and considerably less time.

Cocaine – An illegal drug. Also known as "coke" or "blow," cocaine often resembles a white crystalline or powdery substance. It is highly addictive and dangerous.

Common Application – An application with which students can apply to multiple schools.

Course Registration – The period of official class selection for the upcoming quarter or semester. Prior to registration, it is best to prepare several back-up courses in case a particular class becomes full. If a course is full, students can place themselves on the waitlist, although this still does not guarantee entry.

Division Athletics – Athletic classifications range from Division I to Division III. Division IA is the most competitive, while Division III is considered to be the least competitive.

Dorm – A dorm (or dormitory) is an on-campus housing facility. Dorms can provide a range of options from suite-style rooms to more communal options that include shared bathrooms. Most first-year students live in dorms. Some upperclassmen who wish to stay on campus also choose this option.

Early Action – An application option with which a student can apply to a school and receive an early acceptance response without a binding commitment. This system is becoming less and less available.

Early Decision – An application option that students should use only if they are certain they plan to attend the school in question. If a student applies using the early decision option and is admitted, he or she is required and bound to attend that university. Admission rates are usually higher among students who apply through early decision, as the student is clearly indicating that the school is his or her first choice.

Ecstasy – An illegal drug. Also known as "E" or "X," ecstasy looks like a pill and most resembles an aspirin. Considered a party drug, ecstasy is very dangerous and can be deadly.

Ethernet – An extremely fast Internet connection available in most university-owned residence halls. To use an Ethernet connection properly, a student will need a network card and cable for his or her computer.

Fake ID – A counterfeit identification card that contains false information. Most commonly, students get fake IDs with altered birthdates so that they appear to be older than 21 (and therefore of legal drinking age). Even though it is illegal, many college students have fake IDs in hopes of purchasing alcohol or getting into bars.

Frosh – Slang for "freshman" or "freshmen."

Hazing – Initiation rituals administered by some fraternities or sororities as part of the pledging process. Many universities have outlawed hazing due to its degrading, and sometimes dangerous, nature.

Intramurals (IMs) – A popular, and usually free, sport league in which students create teams and compete against one another. These sports vary in competitiveness and can include a range of activities—everything from billiards to water polo. IM sports are a great way to meet people with similar interests.

Keg – Officially called a half-barrel, a keg contains roughly 200 12-ounce servings of beer.

LSD – An illegal drug, also known as acid, this hallucinogenic drug most commonly resembles a tab of paper.

Marijuana – An illegal drug, also known as weed or pot; along with alcohol, marijuana is one of the most commonly-found drugs on campuses across the country.

Major –The focal point of a student's college studies; a specific topic that is studied for a degree. Examples of majors include physics, English, history, computer science, economics, business, and music. Many students decide on a specific major before arriving on campus, while others are simply "undecided" until declaring a major. Those who are extremely interested in two areas can also choose to double major.

Meal Block – The equivalent of one meal. Students on a meal plan usually receive a fixed number of meals per week. Each meal, or "block," can be redeemed at the school's dining facilities in place of cash. Often, a student's weekly allotment of meal blocks will be forfeited if not used.

Minor – An additional focal point in a student's education. Often serving as a complement or addition to a student's main area of focus, a minor has fewer requirements and prerequisites to fulfill than a major. Minors are not required for graduation from most schools; however some students who want to explore many different interests choose to pursue both a major and a minor.

Mushrooms – An illegal drug. Also known as "'shrooms," this drug resembles regular mushrooms but is extremely hallucinogenic.

Off-Campus Housing – Housing from a particular landlord or rental group that is not affiliated with the university. Depending on the college, off-campus housing can range from extremely popular to non-existent. Students who choose to live off campus are typically given more freedom, but they also have to deal with possible subletting scenarios, furniture, bills, and other issues. In addition to these factors, rental prices and distance often affect a student's decision to move off campus.

Office Hours – Time that teachers set aside for students who have questions about coursework. Office hours are a good forum for students to go over any problems and to show interest in the subject material.

Pledging – The early phase of joining a fraternity or sorority, pledging takes place after a student has gone through rush and received a bid. Pledging usually lasts between one and two semesters. Once the pledging period is complete and a particular student has done everything that is required to become a member, that student is considered a brother or sister. If a fraternity or a sorority would decide to "haze" a group of students, this initiation would take place during the pledging period.

Private Institution – A school that does not use tax revenue to subsidize education costs. Private schools typically cost more than public schools and are usually smaller.

Prof – Slang for "professor."

Public Institution – A school that uses tax revenue to subsidize education costs. Public schools are often a good value for in-state residents and tend to be larger than most private colleges.

Quarter System (or Trimester System) – A type of academic calendar system. In this setup, students take classes for three academic periods. The first quarter usually starts in late September or early October and concludes right before Christmas. The second quarter usually starts around early to mid–January and finishes up around March or April. The last academic quarter, or "third quarter," usually starts in late March or early April and finishes up in late May or Mid-June. The fourth quarter is summer. The major difference between the quarter system and semester system is that students take more, less comprehensive courses under the quarter calendar.

RA (Resident Assistant) – A student leader who is assigned to a particular floor in a dormitory in order to help to the other students who live there. An RA's duties include ensuring student safety and providing assistance wherever possible.

Recitation – An extension of a specific course; a review session. Some classes, particularly large lectures, are supplemented with mandatory recitation sessions that provide a relatively personal class setting.

Rolling Admissions – A form of admissions. Most commonly found at public institutions, schools with this type of policy continue to accept students throughout the year until their class sizes are met. For example, some schools begin accepting students as early as December and will continue to do so until April or May.

Room and Board – This figure is typically the combined cost of a university-owned room and a meal plan.

Room Draw/Housing Lottery – A common way to pick on-campus room assignments for the following year. If a student decides to remain in university-owned housing, he or she is assigned a unique number that, along with seniority, is used to determine his or her housing for the next year.

Rush – The period in which students can meet the brothers and sisters of a particular chapter and find out if a given fraternity or sorority is right for them. Rushing a fraternity or a sorority is not a requirement at any school. The goal of rush is to give students who are serious about pledging a feel for what to expect.

Semester System – The most common type of academic calendar system at college campuses. This setup typically includes two semesters in a given school year. The fall semester starts around the end of August or early September and concludes before winter vacation. The spring semester usually starts in mid-January and ends in late April or May.

Student Center/Rec Center/Student Union – A common area on campus that often contains study areas, recreation facilities, and eateries. This building is often a good place to meet up with fellow students; depending on the school, the student center can have a huge role or a non-existent role in campus life.

Student ID – A university-issued photo ID that serves as a student's key to school-related functions. Some schools require students to show these cards in order to get into dorms, libraries, cafeterias, and other facilities. In addition to storing meal plan information, in some cases, a student ID can actually work as a debit card and allow students to purchase things from bookstores or local shops.

Suite – A type of dorm room. Unlike dorms that feature communal bathrooms shared by the entire floor, suites offer bathrooms shared only among the suite. Suite-style dorm rooms can house anywhere from two to ten students.

TA (Teacher's Assistant) – An undergraduate or grad student who helps in some manner with a specific course. In some cases, a TA will teach a class, assist a professor, grade assignments, or conduct office hours.

Undergraduate – A student in the process of studying for his or her bachelor's degree.

ABOUT THE AUTHOR

This book was a real treat to write. I finally had the opportunity to put my English major to use! Hopefully, this will be the first of many times to come. Running back down memory lane and rehashing the college experience makes me realize how quickly I awoke from the college dream. Now the whole experience seems like it never happened. The dream just swirls together. Take your time at UCLA because working-life holds nothing over college-life (except a paycheck instead of a loan). Although I made my share of memories here, I'd like to think that everyone that picks up this book engages UCLA a little more deeply than I did. If I could tell prospective students to do one thing, I would say study abroad! Regardless of the university that a student chooses to attend, the option to study abroad is golden. Don't miss it! UCLA still is an amazing university for the time that you spend in the United States. What's the one thing I would do at UCLA? Read the book and find out!

Now I send thanks and love to the following: Mommy & Daddy, Ewwwwiiiiiiiinnn (now I turn on the motorbike), Grams (the one and only), Mikel (thanks for the editing help baby cakes), Shearell (you will get your woman), Jon (for being understanding with my job), Uncle Bill & Aunt Rose (I remember the phone call), Delaney (Mr. Santa Fe), Professor Little (for teaching me how to write), Train (buttermil-K, you still sleep funny), Adam (without his computer, this would not be possible), Mike (the brainstorm was a hurricane, and you still sleep real funny), CincoMomo (your help was noticed!), Steve (you never write me back), Sav (you're a little too feisty), the Andersons (just to say I love you all), Rich (for the laughs), Nancy (for the listening), UCLA departments (you know who you are), and to Adam Burns and all of the College Prowler staff for giving me this opportunity!

Erik Robert Flegal
authors@collegeprowler.com

The College Prowler
Big Book of Colleges

Having Trouble Narrowing Down Your Choices?

Try Going Bigger!

BIG BOOK OF COLLEGES '09
7¼" X 10", 1248 Pages Paperback
$29.95 Retail
978-1-4274-0005-5

Choosing the perfect school can be an overwhelming challenge. Luckily, our *Big Book of Colleges* makes that task a little less daunting. We've packed it with overviews of our full library of single-school guides— more than 280 of the nation's top schools—giving you some much-needed perspective on your search.

College Prowler on the Web

Craving some electronic interaction? Check out the new and improved **CollegeProwler.com**! We've included the COMPLETE contents of more than 250 of our single-school guides on the Web—and you can gain access to all of them for just $39.95 per year!

Not only that, but non-subscribers can still view and compare our grades for each school, order books at our online bookstore, or enter our monthly scholarship contest. Don't get left in the dark when making your college decision. Let College Prowler be your guide!

Get the Jolt!

College Jolt gives you a peek behind the scenes

College Jolt is our new blog designed to hook you up with great information, funny videos, cool contests, awesome scholarship opportunities, and honest insight into who we are and what we're all about.

Check us out at ***www.collegejolt.com***

Need Help Paying For School?

Apply for our scholarship!

College Prowler awards thousands of dollars a year to students who compose the best essays. E-mail scholarship@collegeprowler.com for more information, or call 1-800-290-2682.

Apply now at ***www.collegeprowler.com***

Tell Us What Life Is Really Like at Your School!

Have you ever wanted to let people know what your college is really like? Now's your chance to help millions of high school students choose the right college.

Let your voice be heard.

Check out **www.collegeprowler.com** for more info!

Need More Help?

Do you have more questions about this school? Can't find a certain statistic? College Prowler is here to help. We are the best source of college information out there. We have a network of thousands of students who can get the latest information on any school to you ASAP. E-mail us at info@collegeprowler.com with your college-related questions.

E-Mail Us Your College-Related Questions!

Check out *www.collegeprowler.com* for more details.
1-800-290-2682

Write For Us!
Get published! Voice your opinion.

Writing a College Prowler guidebook is both fun and
rewarding; our open-ended format allows your own
creativity free reign. Our writers have been featured
in national newspapers and have seen their names in
bookstores across the country. Now is your chance
to break into the publishing industry with one of the
country's fastest-growing publishers!

Apply now at *www.collegeprowler.com*

Contact editor@collegeprowler.com or
call 1-800-290-2682 for more details.

Pros and Cons

Still can't figure out if this is the right school for you?
You've already read through this in-depth guide;
why not list the pros and cons? It will really help
with narrowing down your decision and determining
whether or not this school is right for you.

Pros	Cons
....	....
....	....
....	....
....	....
....	....
....	....
....	....
....	....
....	....
....	....
....	....
....	....
....	....

Pros and Cons

Still can't figure out if this is the right school for you?
You've already read through this in-depth guide;
why not list the pros and cons? It will really help
with narrowing down your decision and determining
whether or not this school is right for you.

Pros	Cons
....	....
....	....
....	....
....	....
....	....
....	....
....	....
....	....
....	....
....	....
....	....
....	....
....	....

Notes

....

....

....

....

....

....

....

....

....

....

....

....

....

....

Notes

....

....

....

....

....

....

....

....

....

....

....

....

....

....

Notes

....

....

....

....

....

....

....

....

....

....

....

....

....

Notes

....

....

....

....

....

....

....

....

....

....

....

....

....

Notes

....

....

....

....

....

....

....

....

....

....

....

....

....

....

Notes

....

....

....

....

....

....

....

....

....

....

....

....

....

....

Notes

....
....
....
....
....
....
....
....
....
....
....
....
....

Notes

....

....

....

....

....

....

....

....

....

....

....

....

....

....

Notes

....

....

....

....

....

....

....

....

....

....

....

....

....

....

Notes

Notes

....

....

....

....

....

....

....

....

....

....

....

....

....

Notes

Notes

....

....

....

....

....

....

....

....

....

....

....

....

....

....

Notes

....

....

....

....

....

....

....

....

....

....

....

....

....

....

Notes

....

....

....

....

....

....

....

....

....

....

....

....

....

Notes

....

....

....

....

....

....

....

....

....

....

....

....

....

Notes

....

....

....

....

....

....

....

....

....

....

....

....

....

....

Notes

....

....

....

....

....

....

....

....

....

....

....

....

....

....

Notes

....

....

....

....

....

....

....

....

....

....

....

....

....

Notes

....

....

....

....

....

....

....

....

....

....

....

....

....

Notes

Notes

....

....

....

....

....

....

....

....

....

....

....

....

....

Notes

....

....

....

....

....

....

....

....

....

....

....

....

....

Notes

Notes

Notes

Notes

Notes

Notes

....

....

....

....

....

....

....

....

....

....

....

....

....

....

Order now! • collegeprowler.com • 1.800.290.2682
Over 260 single-school guidebooks!

Albion College
Alfred University
Allegheny College
American University
Amherst College
Arizona State University
Auburn University
Babson College
Ball State University
Bard College
Barnard College
Bates College
Baylor University
Beloit College
Bentley College
Binghamton University
Birmingham Southern College
Boston College
Boston University
Bowdoin College
Brandeis University
Brigham Young University
Brown University
Bryn Mawr College
Bucknell University
Cal Poly
Cal Poly Pomona
Cal State Northridge
Cal State Sacramento
Caltech
Carleton College
Carnegie Mellon University
Case Western Reserve
Centenary College of Louisiana
Centre College
Claremont McKenna College
Clark Atlanta University
Clark University
Clemson University
Colby College
Colgate University
College of Charleston
College of the Holy Cross
College of William & Mary
College of Wooster
Colorado College
Columbia University
Connecticut College
Cornell University
Creighton University
CUNY Hunters College
Dartmouth College
Davidson College
Denison University
DePauw University
Dickinson College
Drexel University
Duke University
Duquesne University
Earlham College
East Carolina University
Elon University
Emerson College
Emory University
FIT
Florida State University
Fordham University

Franklin & Marshall College
Furman University
Geneva College
George Washington University
Georgetown University
Georgia Tech
Gettysburg College
Gonzaga University
Goucher College
Grinnell College
Grove City College
Guilford College
Gustavus Adolphus College
Hamilton College
Hampshire College
Hampton University
Hanover College
Harvard University
Harvey Mudd College
Haverford College
Hofstra University
Hollins University
Howard University
Idaho State University
Illinois State University
Illinois Wesleyan University
Indiana University
Iowa State University
Ithaca College
IUPUI
James Madison University
Johns Hopkins University
Juniata College
Kansas State
Kent State University
Kenyon College
Lafayette College
LaRoche College
Lawrence University
Lehigh University
Lewis & Clark College
Louisiana State University
Loyola College in Maryland
Loyola Marymount University
Loyola University Chicago
Loyola University New Orleans
Macalester College
Marlboro College
Marquette University
McGill University
Miami University of Ohio
Michigan State University
Middle Tennessee State
Middlebury College
Millsaps College
MIT
Montana State University
Mount Holyoke College
Muhlenberg College
New York University
North Carolina State
Northeastern University
Northern Arizona University
Northern Illinois University
Northwestern University
Oberlin College
Occidental College

Ohio State University
Ohio University
Ohio Wesleyan University
Old Dominion University
Penn State University
Pepperdine University
Pitzer College
Pomona College
Princeton University
Providence College
Purdue University
Reed College
Rensselaer Polytechnic Institute
Rhode Island School of Design
Rhodes College
Rice University
Rochester Institute of Technology
Rollins College
Rutgers University
San Diego State University
Santa Clara University
Sarah Lawrence College
Scripps College
Seattle University
Seton Hall University
Simmons College
Skidmore College
Slippery Rock
Smith College
Southern Methodist University
Southwestern University
Spelman College
St. Joseph's University Philkadelphia
St. John's University
St. Louis University
St. Olaf College
Stanford University
Stetson University
Stony Brook University
Susquehanna University
Swarthmore College
Syracuse University
Temple University
Tennessee State University
Texas A & M University
Texas Christian University
Towson University
Trinity College Connecticut
Trinity University Texas
Truman State
Tufts University
Tulane University
UC Berkeley
UC Davis
UC Irvine
UC Riverside
UC San Diego
UC Santa Barbara
UC Santa Cruz
UCLA
Union College
University at Albany
University at Buffalo
University of Alabama
University of Arizona
University of Central Florida
University of Chicago

University of Colorado
University of Connecticut
University of Delaware
University of Denver
University of Florida
University of Georgia
University of Illinois
University of Iowa
University of Kansas
University of Kentucky
University of Maine
University of Maryland
University of Massachusetts
University of Miami
University of Michigan
University of Minnesota
University of Mississippi
University of Missouri
University of Nebraska
University of New Hampshire
University of North Carolina
University of Notre Dame
University of Oklahoma
University of Oregon
University of Pennsylvania
University of Pittsburgh
University of Puget Sound
University of Rhode Island
University of Richmond
University of Rochester
University of San Diego
University of San Francisco
University of South Carolina
University of South Dakota
University of South Florida
University of Southern California
University of Tennessee
University of Texas
University of Utah
University of Vermont
University of Virginia
University of Washington
University of Wisconsin
UNLV
Ursinus University
Valparaiso University
Vanderbilt University
Vassar College
Villanova University
Virginia Tech
Wake Forest University
Warren Wilson College
Washington and Lee University
Washington University in St. Louis
Wellesley College
Wesleyan University
West Point
West Virginia University
Wheaton College IL
Wheaton College MA
Whitman College
Wilkes University
Williams College
Xavier University
Yale University

Breinigsville, PA USA
25 April 2010
236716BV00004B/2/P